TRVTH HVRTS

DEFEATING THE ENEMY WITHIN

RIDWAN AZIZ

First Printing 2019
First Edition 2019

ISBN 9781687513496

10 9 8 7 6 5 4 3 2 1

Copies are available at special rates for bulk orders.
Contact the sales development team at trvthhvrts@outlook.com for
more information.

TRVTH HVRTS

Table of Contents

Prologue

Take a minute, appreciate and come to the realisation that each random passerby is living a life as vivid and as complex as your own- populated with their own ambitions, friends, routines, worries and inherited craziness- an epic story that continues invisibly around you like an anthill sprawling deep underground, with elaborate passageways to thousands of other lives that you'll never know existed, in which you might appear only once, as an extra sipping coffee in the background, as a blur of traffic passing a highway, as a lighted window at dusk.

This is life. You pass by different energies every day; you only connect with a few those who spark and ignite a feeling between the two of you resulting in a relationship and ultimately a bond. We are all individuals facing our own trials and tribulations but this is all a part of our journey. Your story is unique to you. You must remain resilient and not be disheartened when others aren't as compassionate, ambitious, loving and motivated as you. Life involves different energies on different callings.

RIDWAN AZIZ

Introduction

We are all distinctive individuals so this book isn't something which is a one size fits all or something that will be able to solve all of your problems since we are all non-identical with our own ways of life; we are all entitled to our own opinions and we will all have differences amongst each other however these differences in beliefs and culture make us who we are and being able to accept and embrace these differences teaches us to view things from alternative perspectives. To quote Aristotle: "It is the mark of an educated mind to be able to entertain a thought without accepting it." We can choose to appreciate the aspects of belief that others hold and appreciate where they stand in regard to a variety of topics without necessarily adopting or supporting what they stand for. Often we shut off our minds due to pride and because of this, our minds will never grow. Remember that our ignorance only limits our awareness; awareness is the fundamental principle to growth and this goes for self-awareness and awareness of one's surroundings and environment.

The reader may be able to relate to some of this book's content and hopefully, learn valuable lessons and wisdom from the mistakes made by the different people mentioned in this book to an extent that they can implement the knowledge they've gained. That being said we have to be able to analyse situations and not be fixed in our approach to dilemmas because in one scenario a certain reaction may be appropriate but in another similar scenario, there may be other factors at play which need to be considered hence resulting in a different approach being applied. This book does not claim to be exhaustive as it would be nearly impossible to look at all the possible variables when it comes to self-development and consciousness especially in relation to people and their behaviours.

It is important to differentiate between information and knowledge. Information is the facts learned about something whilst knowledge is an advancement on the information learned- to a point where one has information pertaining to a certain matter and then goes and takes the extra step by applying what they have learned. Everyone who is knowledgeable is well informed but not everyone who is well informed is knowledgeable and the reason being is when knowledge is practiced it allows one to experience things for themselves and from those experiences they can learn; they learn what they did correct and what are invaluable lessons and what was a mistake teaching them not to repeat those same mistakes or to adapt their approach in regards to that situation. Experience over time leads to wisdom which is where one is blessed with the quality of making sensible judgements; this is a position which we should all strive to achieve and a characteristic which we should desire to acquire because with wisdom we are able to make decisions which benefit us as we are able to weigh up different variables- the advantages and the consequences of an action.

This book had two intentions in mind when being written. The first was to allow the reader to understand themselves and their own value and the second to teach the reader how to operate themselves in their environment and how to approach different situations. So, in essence, the book addresses two different things throughout: self and environment. We have included a series of theoretical cases and real-life scenarios where the lessons we mention in this book have been applied or had the potential to be applied. Most of this book is based on personal experiences, vicarious experiences, and stories as well as knowledge acquired from various mentors and teachers. The names of the people mentioned in this book have been changed for the protection of their identity and out of respect for their confidentiality.

This is a self-help book and by the end of it, the reader should have the necessary tools and information to better themselves in regard to their character development and their consciousness concerning their environment. They will have the necessary information on how to carry themselves as a positive energy source. At the end of the day, everything in life is energy. There is good energy, bad energy, and balanced/ neutral energy. We may experience fluctuations in our energy levels and this goes for mentally and well as physically and the most favourable energy to us is positive good energy. The law of conservation of energy states that: "Energy can neither be created nor destroyed; energy can only be transferred or changed from one form to another." We interact with people on a daily basis and our energies are at work, in tandem, and although we are not directly responsible for the actions and energies put out by others we can have an indirect effect and influence on others leading to their change as well as our own. Every individual has the same twenty-four hours and we are all just as capable as each other to shoot our shots, aim for our dreams and materialise those dreams. The objective and dream of this book is to help develop us into an aware and conscious being that can live a life of contentment in a world that has grown to be toxic and unappreciative at times.

Anyways before we delve further into these topics it may be necessary to put out a disclaimer and make clear that this book in no way is a medical or scientific article although may contain elements of the two. This book may take form as therapy for some but with anything we do, we do not intend nor imply this as a substitute for professional advice, it has been provided for educational purposes only as a hope to improve lives even if it's an improvement by the slightest.

Mindset

Mindset is everything.

A mindset is an established set of attitudes that you hold. Your mindset includes a collection of thoughts and beliefs which shape your habits which then has an effect on your lifestyle and this is because your mindset impacts the way that you view the world and how you make sense of it. Mindsets are built then reinforced but they always have the potential to grow, expand and adapt. They can help you understand yourself, revealing the way you predetermine your responses and interpretations of situations. There two basic types of mindsets which are: a fixed mindset and a growth mindset. The correct mindset can help you better achieve the various goals and objectives you set yourself, as the mind is a powerful tool that has control over you and your decisions. The average human makes on average 35,000 decisions a day and the better decisions you make, the better the outcomes you get.

Carol Dweck explains that someone with a fixed mindset is someone who believes intelligence is static. These people have a desire to look smart and therefore they have a tendency to avoid challenges, give up easily when facing obstacles and are fearful of not being perceived in a positive way. This type of person is likely to plateau early and achieve less than their full potential. Meanwhile, someone with a growth mindset believes that intelligence can be developed. These people have a desire to learn and therefore have a tendency to embrace the challenges they encounter and persist and endure through the setbacks they face. This type of person has the potential to reach and exceed the levels of achievement that they could've never have imagined. If it isn't obvious you should look to have a growth mindset assuming you are looking to achieve a lot and are an ambitious individual.

Intentions form a large part of our mindset. You know yourself better than anyone else does. You know your reasoning and logic behind why you do certain actions, the motivation behind doing them and the consequences of not doing them. You know the severity of what's at stake. You know your intentions and whether they are sincere or not. Insincerity is a sin and a form of negative energy because when we are insincere we lack genuine reasoning and we look to acquire things for the wrong reasons; it may even result in us acting immorally but we must remember that wrong is wrong even if everyone else is doing it and right is right even if nobody else is doing it. Purify your intentions so that you won't have a conscious to clear in the future. Speak to those who have gone through similar paths to you and have achieved the success that you desire to achieve and they will tell you the reality of it. You will find that when you have acquired money, money doesn't impress you or when you've been partying, that gets old. This is because you are a subject to a particular lifestyle, that factor in your life which was once so important diminishes in value over time so chasing the illusions others are chasing after proves rather futile because you will not be doing things for you and you will not be doing things with a purpose. So instead try utilising your energy properly as this will better benefit you, aiding you on your journey to achieving a level of fulfilment and contentment. Money does not equate to happiness necessarily. Money is important but not everything. You could spend thousands of pounds on designer clothes and shoes yet you are still the same person you always were. Change is initiated within oneself and how they change their environment because that is what causes growth and causes their perspective and outlook to change. This doesn't mean you should not look to acquire wealth or enjoy yourself by satisfying your needs and desires but you should be able to logically justify your behaviour not to just anyone but more importantly to yourself.

When talking about the reasoning behind our actions it isn't only to do with new actions but our habits as well. People fall into toxic behaviours all of the time however what makes the difference between those who remain toxic and those that cleanse themselves is the renewal of intentions and resilience to being defined by their toxic traits. One may fall into the habit of toxic behaviour but as long as they identify that toxicity and attempt to deal with it then it is only a matter of time until that toxic habit it unlearned and a good habit is developed. What you don't want to happen is for you to get so used to your own toxic behaviours and accept them due to the fact you've given up trying to address them. In many Asian, South American and even African cultures it is common practice to eat with one's hands so imagine eating something for breakfast that requires your hands it will ultimately lead to your hands getting messy and the same happens for lunch and then dinner, your hands get messy with food all over them, this doesn't mean that you are messy person and you don't think that since you are messy now you won't wash your hands clean since you will get messy again. No, instead, you wash your hands. In the same way after every action you do complete you wash your hands cleaning yourselves from your flaws and toxicity.

To create an ideal positive mindset you need to clear your mind and detox it from negativity. Some of us are wired to focus on the negative or to keep playing back old narratives in our heads. Concentrate on trying to untangle that mess and feed your mind what you want to focus on about yourself. Do a detox for your mind and you can do this by writing down the good thoughts you want to think of yourself on a piece of paper, read out these statements to yourself, aloud, and repeat it over and over again until those positive thoughts are rooted in your mind. This way you are substituting the negative thoughts with good thoughts. Life can be stressful with thousands of thoughts running through your mind and with hundreds of tasks on your to-do list in need of completion. It can take a mental strain on you which in turn takes a heavy tax on your mental well-being and even your physical self. Focusing on self-care is a powerful way of becoming your best self. You are your own main priority. In situations of stress and anxiety, it may be effective to practice mindfulness to clear your headspace. Mindfulness is a mental state achieved by focusing on one's awareness on the present moment, while calmly acknowledging and accepting one's feelings and thoughts. This provides useful because it clears your mind from all extra information and allows you to focus on your priorities. When maintaining mindfulness we don't rehearse the past neither do we imagine the future. Mindfulness allows you to remain calm and at ease. Calmness is a state of trust. When you are calm about everything it allows your mind to explore ideas freely and find solutions. When you aren't calm then you are most likely over-thinking and have a higher tendency to overreact. Allow yourself to surrender for that moment whether it is through prayer, meditation or experiencing a serene moment of peace. Allow yourself to gather your thoughts and receive guidance. Mindfulness allows you to not take everything to heart and hold onto sanity because you understand that will exhaust you and waste your energy. You should frequently rest yourself not only in the literal, physical sense but emotionally and psychologically. Some experts estimate that the human mind thinks between 60,000 to 80,000 thoughts per day and of those thoughts it is believed that 98% of them are exactly the same thoughts we have the previous day. This means if you were to face a predicament the negative thoughts related to it will continue to obsess your mind; this teaches us when we are hurt we shouldn't ignore the pain but tend to it. We should seek the root cause of that suffering, not just the symptoms. The goal is to rise and move forward.

Movement is how we as animals stay alive. In the jungle, it's the swiftest and most diligent that survives because if an animal were to stay still they would fall victim to prey. Life is filled with different phases and periods just because you are currently in the darkness doesn't mean you will stay in the darkness because the night always comes to an end and the sun does eventually rise again. It is mandatory for you to move forward and keep changing otherwise you will not be able to achieve your potential and progress. Imagine still being at the mental capability of a toddler, then ask yourself, would you be able to do half the things that you do? The answer is quite obviously no. Change is a sign of growth and evolution. For anything to carry on living it needs to evolve. The only thing that doesn't grow is a dead person. Often people claim "I've never changed" or "I'm still the same old person" thinking it's something praiseworthy but in reality, it is far from that. If you are not changing on a daily basis in a mental, physical, financial and/ or spiritual sense then you are slowly killing yourself and failing yourself as a living being. Growth is about transcending to different levels so you can interact with new opportunities and since you have dedicated yourself to change you might as well change as dramatically as possible. This means set big goals for yourself because even if you don't achieve those goals you are aiming higher and pushing your capacity. When you set the bar low for yourself you will just do what is required of you. In that case, you are settling for less than you deserve and getting the bare minimum. Have high aspirations and the utmost belief in yourself. There is nothing cocky about believing in your ability. There is a distinct line partitioning confidence and cockiness. Ambition should be energy that can be channelled not to inspire just you but those around you.

Every journey is filled with hills and valleys, highs and lows, ups and downs. A part of having a strong mindset is being able to bounce back from losses without becoming heartless and being able to hold on to some degree of compassion. Believe in chance and that there will be an abundance of opportunities. When a person faces rejection their self-confidence gets shattered. If you allow rejection to affect you, you limit your potential because your self-esteem has taken a knock but with an abundance mindset, you always look for the new and the next opportunity so you will always have possibilities. If something doesn't turn out the way you wanted it isn't the end of the world and is actually far from it. If you search hard enough there is often another opportunity and perhaps that opportunity will work better than your initial plan, so you don't need to drown in pain and sorrow. The pain you feel from a situation is nothing but the lesson you need to look deeper the next time so that history doesn't repeat itself. We can't get stung in the same place twice or by the same person twice. The pain that you felt leads to the lesson you needed to learn because how else would you have learned that lesson? You wouldn't have unless you know of someone who has already been through a situation similar. The saying by Stephen King goes: "Fool me one-time shame on you, fool two times shame on me." If you see no good in anybody that is not a result of there not being good in others; it is a result of a flawed outlook and perspective on your part. This is profound from a leadership standpoint, on either a domestic scale as a parent who manages a household or a larger scale as a leader who oversees a nation, because if we lack belief in those we are serving because we think that they are undeserving of our services then we become a liability, not them. This is because we are failing to fulfil the rights of those who are entitled and deserving of them. It makes us incapable of serving due to the pessimism anchoring us. On your journey of self-development, you will go through every emotion there is. You will find you have moments where you are seen as motivation to others around you and at this level, you are seen a source of inspiration for others; you can achieve this level quicker if you keep self-educating and learning as this will open your eyes to new experiences. Always learn from the people before you, before you become an example for those that come after you. Experience can be the best of teachers and mistakes can mould you to become a strong person. However, the truly wise person uses the mistakes of those before them as a guide to avoid mistakes in their own life. That being said there needs to be a consonance between your intentions and your speech, then between your speech and actions. The blind can't lead the blind so be about the life that you preach.

One thing that has a key influence on our mental processing and perception is our diet. Our diet is everything that we consume as individuals and it is not restricted to what we eat. Diet accounts for what we eat, what we listen to and what we watch because all of these play a factor in the person we are and the behaviours we portray. Consuming yourself in things that are poor for your physical and mental health will result in negative behaviour. If you feed yourself with brain-stimulating material and things that are considered good for your health this will correlate with your behaviour. The most effective way to change your life is by changing the way that you think and approach problems. You don't get good fruit off a bad tree. If your headspace is somewhere negative the ideas that you produce and the suggestions that you contribute will not be of quality and benefit.

Another thing we can do to improve our mind frame and mental processing is taking caution in the way we talk to ourselves. Language plays a big factor in our mental processing and our perception. This is due to schemas we associate certain words. Words have different connotations with different levels of severity and effect. So by simply changing the way we structure statements and the words we use when asking ourselves questions, we can significantly change our way of mental processing. This means over time due to our subconscious programming, we will have changed positively in regards to self-talk. For instance, as opposed to being limited by "I can't do…" and "I won't be able to…" statements we should try finding solutions by asking questions like "How can I…?" or use "I am" statements. This creates a stronger mind, one with an internal locus of control where we take more accountability and responsibility for our outcomes in life, our actions, and their consequences. One technique which we can use to achieve our objectives is one where we take what we want and break it down into micro-steps needed to achieve that goal. Language can be of two types: convictional or conditional. Convictional words are words of declaration such as "will, surely, do," these words are convincing you to take action as opposed to conditional words which are words that are subject to another variable such as "if, maybe, attempt." Commanding yourself to do something will more likely encourage you to do it because you leave zero room for 'no'. The removal of conditional words from your vocabulary is something that will boost your productivity and help you take the necessary steps to progress towards your respected goals.

Growth, progression, and elevation are things we hear about a lot but are you truly fit for that grind. It takes discipline, dedication, and determination. It by no means is something easy and it can be a long process in which you will end up in you losing a lot of your friends and sacrificing other elements of your social life but the rewards can be great. You can't feel bad for outgrowing people that had a chance to grow with you. It is okay to be unwilling to interact with certain characters too. It doesn't mean you are anti-social or it isn't a sign of dispute because all you are doing is doing what is best for you. It is said that to elevate it is necessary that one separates from others so they can evolve themselves and direct their energy for progress. You may feel as though you are forcing yourself to be an introvert because of your lifestyle but then you begin to enjoy being alone but it turns out to be that you really like being at peace with yourself and in your zone with your own company. This doesn't mean you've become hostile and detached because you find you are still extremely extroverted with people who bring you comfort and happiness.

A development in mindset isn't an assassination of your character but a journey of learning, adaption, and improvement which leads to a strengthened persona. When people see that you change your life they don't realise that you can still be the same person. You still hold yourself to the same principles. You are the same person whether in track pants and a t-shirt or a suit. When you are able to out-think your surroundings you see growth. If your surroundings prove limiting it is most often a lack of ambition and drive with those people and it may not be their fault but because their mindset is fixed and conditioned by culture and their education or lack of education for that matter. However, you can't get overwhelmed by what seems to be an obstacle. Don't focus too much on the obstacles and don't put too much emphasis on them either. If you only focus on the obstacles then you can't step back, look from different perspectives and strategically think. You blind yourself from seeing the course of action it takes to overcome those obstacles.

Change can be quite a daunting experience but suppress those emotions of fear, doubt, and anxiety. Changing doesn't mean becoming the total opposite of what you were and what you stood for but it means adapting. Switching is when you adopt the antithesis of what you once were and switching up is rarely a good thing if it means you ditch the morals and principles and beliefs that you strongly held. Feed yourself things which will help you grow and develop or else you will end up dead whether it means unwell and slowly heading towards your deathbed or in the other sense living life braindead. You are required to stay driven as an individual; motivation is temporary and short-term but drive is long-term and lasting. When you are driven you are focused and ready to knock out any obstacles in your way. Motivation is a feeling that comes and goes. Drive is always there, yes, it can be higher at some points and lower at others but it is always there meaning that every day you are always making progress whether it be baby steps or huge strides forward.

Once you achieve the change you need or desire you'll need to maintain it so you don't go back to the negative ways you previously were and so you can carry on latching yourself to positivity. A wise man once said conquering is easy but ruling is not so easy. We may achieve an accomplish something but may struggle to uphold it; let alone let it develop, grow and flourish. One can get married yet not be able to have a successful marriage. One can acquire wealth but fail to manage it. A tribe may win a battle but may not be qualified to govern the land. When it comes to developing a strong mindset we will eventually develop good habits however what is the most important thing is being able to maintain those habits and not relapse and go back to our old selves.

Accountability

Nothing changes if nothing changes. Everybody desires change and changing for the better however the fact of the matter is that people are not willing to deal with their root problems and take the necessary actions and steps to solve them; instead, individuals may develop a victim mindset or be in denial of their problems. When someone has an addiction it is said that the first step is admitting that they have a problem, although this is true of addiction it is also true of life and life's adversities in general. One may fix the symptom but not the real, root problem. One will perpetuate their toxicities without realising they're doing so. We don't understand why we continue ending up back in the same toxic spaces. The reason being is that we're forever treating the symptoms believing that we've cured the issue at hand only to have our problems later manifest in one way or another. We have to solve the root issues in order to heal. Many of our issues in adulthood stem from childhood trauma. One may be a drug abuser or an alcoholic but these are just symptoms of a person's problem. The real problem may be the person is facing depression or trying to escape their reality. We need to accept our flaws and own up to our toxic behaviours and proclaim our desire to change by outlining exactly what we will do to sort out the problems at hand. The easiest thing to do is displace these problems on to somebody or something else but that doesn't deal with the root issue and inevitably new problems will stem and arise like branches from a tree trunk. Time and time again people have proven they are able to talk the talk but only a select few can truly walk the walk. Self-improvement starts internally by improving our hearts, conscious and our mentality after these factors are in a positive state then change becomes dramatically easier because as individuals we are no longer bound by our ignorance or our negative thought processes which therein unlocks us to new undiscovered potentials. Arguably the majority of us are slaves, not physically but mentally, and the hardest prison to escape is our own mind because due to our sub-conscious and prior experiences, we determine our own ability and all too often we underestimate ourselves and our potential. For instance, you may go to work out in the gym deciding to do an exercise set of twelve reps, already you have subconsciously limited what you can achieve because you're subconsciously telling yourself that you are only capable of that volume and nothing more; what may even happen is that you'll begin to make excuses for yourself midway through the exercise meaning you won't even try to achieve what you initially planned out to achieve. All too often, our self-diagnosis is too strict and we are capable of far more than we think in a lot of cases. Humans overestimate what they can achieve in a day and they underestimate what they can achieve in a lifetime.

You may find yourself in a position of doubt and scepticism creating every excuse there is in the book so you don't have to tend the issues at core and rebuild yourself because that requires change, which is not easy whatsoever, as it requires you to explore your fears, enter new territories and fall into an abyss of unfamiliarity. However, if you don't take action when will you? You will always come up with reasons not to change and so you remain seemingly content deep in your comfort zone. You must convince yourself to take action immediately because if you do what you've always done, you'll get what you've always got as the same actions result in the same outcomes. Is it one day or day one when it comes to achieving your ideal self and unlocking your true identity? When conversing with anyone elderly they will most likely mention their regrets in life for not taking this risk or not doing that activity or learning that skill. It would be a shame to drown in emotions of sorrow and regret because you didn't utilise your life in a way that would truly please you. You would regret your decisions of sticking by people who never really loved you, doing things that you really didn't like doing and putting your own interests last in the name of selflessness and companionship.

In order to achieve change, there will have to be a level of sacrifice. There is an opportunity cost where you choose to invest in your self-development which will benefit you in the long-term but in turn, you risk leaving your comfort zone and what you are familiar with and accustomed to. Routines will get broken and new ones will be created but you shouldn't look to sabotage your greatness due to your reluctance in taking opportunities. We all fear the unknown and the new challenges we could face but it's time to embrace it and accept the challenges as that will make us move closer to greatness even if it means exploring new avenues; what you need to know most will be found where you least want to look. It can be the scariest thing right before making the transition to the next level because it requires risk and sacrifice; perhaps you temporarily lose everything to achieve that greatness. Sacrifice is not pleasant but you need to get in a habit of asking yourself "does this support the life I'm trying to create?" when it comes to trying new things. Although you may endure pain in the short-run surely the benefits exceed the costs in the long-term. Tough situations ultimately build strong people.

There will never be a perfect time to start. You may not know the perfect way to do things but through accumulating experience you learn and find what works for you. Starting now and building over time will exceed the advantages of waiting for the so-called right time to start because the ideal time may never come. Nobody is perfect and we are all subject to our own faults. It is okay to admit that we are wrong in some situations or we may be unable to do something but what is important is how we will get it right the next time. Failure is something guaranteed and inevitable however failure isn't a problem unless it affects our ability to function and conduct daily mundane activities. Failure is the best teacher that you could ever wish for because it humbles you and enables you to find out what doesn't work; which leaves you closer to finding out what does work for you. Failure allows for introspection. It is never too late to change and better yourself. We as individuals should seek to and strive to reach a level of self-contentment and happiness through a gradual and progressive transformation so that we can have a positive impact maybe not on a major scale but at least on a level where we are responsible for positive influences due to our interactions with those that we encounter on a regular basis. Life is like operating a start-up business. You learn a little bit and implement it to test to see if it works and then you keep iterating it until it is closer to perfection. You are in essence creating a customised system for yourself. Learn, adapt, live!

Choices are conscious decisions that we make in order to achieve a certain objective. Choices are the fundamental of anything and everything, as they are responsible for the actions we conduct. By honing our decision-making ability to opt for the better choice we achieve our objectives quickly and effectively. Everything we do is a choice from brushing our teeth in the morning to eating throughout the day to preparing ourselves to go to sleep. Everything is a choice. Giving is a choice. Honesty is a choice. Optimism is a choice. Happiness is a choice. Forgiveness is a choice. The words we speak are a choice. Teaching others is a choice. Respecting others is a choice. Showing gratitude is a choice. When push comes to shove smart people make better choices. A choice is either a step in the right direction or the wrong direction. A series of choices will lead you progressively closer or further from your goal. Humans are creatures of habit; we make choices and continue to make them hence a habit is formed and this determines the direction we head in and is a good indicator of our final outcome. A single choice will not ruin everything nor lead to overnight success in the large majority of cases however a series of choices will have an impact on what happens in our lives. Choices that are done consistently over a period of time develop into habits which are things we do naturally due to our conditioning. Our actions become habits and our habits become our reality. You don't become overweight by overeating once; you don't live paycheck to paycheck by overspending once; you don't have bad credit by missing a payment once; you don't have relationship issues by not communicating once. You should take accountability for your situation and take the necessary steps to develop good habits and reduce your bad habits because this will determine your lifestyle and reality in the future. Remember, you only end up in very bad places one step at a time so you must watch the steps you are taking.

Despite saying all that change doesn't happen overnight. You shouldn't be harsh on yourself and beat yourself up when you do something you told yourself you wouldn't do. When it comes to change the initial stage in familiarising yourself with what is a good habit and then the application comes after. You may be impatient in your approach, trying to achieve a year's progress in a day's work, and yes, it is true we will achieve some progress but you don't want to collapse your program due to stress and over-working yourself. Small consistent steps in the right direction are significantly more effective than one large leap every once in a while. Your journey and development may not go as planned and intended due to complications you didn't account for but you must stay committed to your decisions yet stay flexible in your approach. When you set out to accomplish something you don't change the goal but always adapt the plan. Development takes management. You need to be able to manage yourself under different conditions. To manage is when you are able to organise your activities so that you can fulfil to your specific obligations and achieve your goals. If you are able to successfully manage your energy throughout the day you can correctly go about your business, which in essence is the activity of life. Business is a transaction where one person exchanges one thing for another, this doesn't necessarily have to be a tangible good or money but it also can be in regard to exchanging your time and energy with someone. Any business takes planning. When in the pursuit of perfection success can only occur if your moves are premeditated as proper preparation prevents piss-poor performance. Nothing should surprise you as everything should be anticipated. When planning to achieve something you should approach it with a degree of preparation. If you have no understanding of accountability you will not plan or acknowledge where you need to improve and ultimately you will not achieve your goals.

A good level of accountability is fundamental when it comes to being a successful person who looks to achieve great things. To be accountable is to take responsibility for your own actions. Accountability is where you take the blame for the mistakes that you've made, understanding that the events that occurred were down to you and your lack of judgement. Accountability is where you hold yourself responsible for the things that you said you were going to do or the things that you were going to keep away from. Accountability eliminates the time wasted dwelling on distracting things and liberates time for you to work more productively. As someone who looks to take charge of your life and become a leader, accountability is crucial as it helps you build character through resilience as opposed to displacing the fault and putting the blame on your peers and others. We all have two hands: the upper hand and the lower hand. The upper hand is one which gives and the lower hand is one which receives. A strong person will always have a stronger upper hand because they aren't reliant on others to get things done for them as they have built and developed themselves so they can independently do things and accomplish their goals. A person who always takes, takes, takes is not honourable and has no morals and principles and wouldn't survive on their own two feet.

We are looking to become independent, self-sufficient individuals and this requires us to fix our mindset which includes our position on the locus of control. The locus of control is a continuum showing the degree to which people believe that they have control over the outcome of events in their lives as opposed to external forces that are beyond their control. On one end we have an internal locus of control where an individual takes full responsibility for the outcome of events in their lives and on the other end we have an external locus of control where an individual believes that others and their environment are responsible for the outcome of events in their life whether it be success or failure. You are looking to be at a level that is closer towards an internal locus of control- where you are taking accountability for your actions and their consequences but allow some leniency for events that you cannot directly control and have little significant influence over. You may find yourselves fixating on the results and outcome of something but that cannot be controlled directly. Yes, you should begin a journey with the end in mind but a part of accountability is taking control and focusing on what you can change whether it is risk, cost, time or behaviour. An entrepreneur may be innovative a create a product which is completely revolutionary but their focus will be on the number of sales they can make and how much profit they can take home instead they can maximise profits more effectively through better brand building, the mitigation of risks and the minimisation costs so the things which provide higher value to the end-user. They can't exactly determine the return they'll make only forecast it.

Life is filled with energy which has been around long before you were even birthed into this world and with all this energy at work. Some people are in more favourable positions over others not necessarily because of luck but because of their actions and behaviours as well as the actions and behaviours of their ancestors. Their ancestors worked hard in order to create a generational impact. They had the ability to better utilise these energies and resources. Life isn't fair; it was never fair and never will be fair because you don't have control over the external energies at work but what you do have control over is your energy. The energy that you carry and emit it, that energy has power which can then have an influence on your surroundings. Some things may serve the purpose of guiding us towards a certain direction somewhat like a symbol whether it is something we see or a person we meet. These things or people serve as nothing but a connection, to attract your attention and motivate you to serve your purpose; they are not a source of energy. It is your own personal responsibility to re-adjust your lens and navigate your life accordingly to begin fulfilling a worthy human experience.

Take ownership of yourself; take ownership of your life. You should do things for yourself because at the end of the day it will be you who has to deal with the consequences of your actions whether they are rewards or problems. Once you begin to realise that you have the power to change your situation you tap into your self-worth because you finally recognise your power to create an effect in your life. Stop giving away your agency and take accountability and responsibility to fix whatever problem you've come to face otherwise you will be left in the same position with no development yet have continuous negativity flowing your veins and entitlement you think you deserve. Entitlement is a disease. People who are entitled tend to be complainers. History repeats itself. You could be facing a certain dilemma at the moment and think there's no way out of it but there is and all it requires is a bit of problem-solving. Someone was in the same situation as you and managed to overcome it. It's not about what befalls you, it's about how you react to and deal with what befalls you. Don't feel sorry for yourself especially if you're involved in business and entrepreneurship as you can't afford to feel sorry for yourself because in that life your position revolves around you being a leader. This life is sink or swim. If you feel sorry for yourself it has an impact on your team and then overall productivity will fall. The business world and the markets don't care about your personal situation. Yes, tend to your pain and take the necessary steps to heal yourself but until you are healed don't jump too quickly things because you will end up doing more damage than progress. You are not only responsible for yourself but you are responsible for the things you engage in and businesses you run which then branches out into a lot of other smaller operations whether it be different sectors or different workers which need to be overseen; the same can be said about relationships don't go entering a relationship filled with pain because you'll only end up damaging the other person and they haven't done anything to deserve the trauma and poor experience you'll take them through.

Self-Discipline

Awareness is a perceptive skill where one has knowledge of their situation. Once an individual is aware they can expand their horizons as they are conscious of their purpose, habits and their surroundings; with awareness, they can set their goals and objectives as well as analyse the obstacles they may encounter and through discipline and determination, they can go about fulfilling these goals. We need to be aware of everything. We need to be aware of current affairs. We need to be aware of people and how they behave. We need to be aware of how we use and acquire our wealth in whatever form it comes.

One aspect of awareness is being realistic. Each person is unique with their own different skill sets, with different things they are good at and specialise in. Everybody has their calling and one may find theirs through exploring and experimenting with different things. However, one may try and force their calling and continuously attempt to achieve something and find no success in it for them. Sometimes knowing when to quit will save you not only time and effort but mental well-being because attempting something which isn't for you over time may manifest into a self-destructive nature in you which consequences in troubles with other activities which you engage in. To live your life perceptually will bring you awareness and with that awareness, you can invest your time effectively in a way that gives you the best return on investment with rewards such as happiness and contentment. In today's capitalist world people invest their time chasing what they think is wealth which is money and power to them, however, truthfully wealth is of four types:

- Financial wealth (money)
- Social wealth (status)
- Time wealth (freedom)
- Physical wealth (health)

A lot of the time society defines wealth by the first two and hence we do the most to chase those at the expense and sacrifice of the latter two. It is important to take care of yourself because if you were to die today, your job vacancy will be posted online before your obituary. We may overwork ourselves causing ourselves to be stressed and drained which has a direct effect on our mental health and as the severity increases of these complications our physical health is also affected. Health is truly wealth because it is our minds responsible for creating options and making the decisions that we mentioned are important in the previous chapters.

Self-discipline is nothing but having awareness and control over you and your actions by avoiding bad habits however tempting they are and developing good ones however objectionable they are because sticking to the good habits which will lead you to success. Success is nothing but the sum of small efforts repeated; little bite-size pieces of hard work over a timespan will equate to success. There are a number of ways to be successful so no one can give you the direct path to success but having discipline is common amongst all successful people. Having a high level of discipline is about self-control which means developing your brain to consciously choose the options which will be ultimately beneficial for you further down the line even if it requires taking the longer and harder route. It is easy to take drugs and do nothing for hours. It is easy to lose your mind over a relationship obsessing over someone that doesn't want you. It is easy to joke on and criticise other people. However, it is not easy to go outside and make something from nothing. It is not easy to do the exact opposite of what everyone else is doing. It is not easy sacrificing the time you value to build and create something that you, your family and friends can all benefit from. Your mind is a terrible thing to waste, use it to be productive. Don't allow yourself to take the easy way out no matter how tempting it is. It takes resilience and patience. Patience is a virtue which in turn builds character. In life, you will be tested in so many different ways going through trials and hardship and whilst going through them you'd think to yourself that this is the hardest thing that you've ever faced. You will feel betrayed and hurt; you will sometimes see no way out of your problems. Patience is one of the most important things one can learn to have especially if they don't have it because patience allows time to analyse and think. Patience is something which is attained and without it, you lack foundation which leaves you with the likelihood of falling apart into pieces.

Discipline starts off with the understanding of the concept of rewards and consequences. This allows a person to make a choice and realise its implications. You can visualise the effects of going with one option over the other and you can then decide which path you want to take. Being a person of discipline always leads to rewards and once you get the ball rolling you become a force to reckon with because you achieve the tasks you set for yourself and it becomes routine for you because you develop new habits and you become addicted to the small scale successes. However keeping disciplined is a challenge, it requires sacrifice. You have to ask yourself what distractions are you willing to give up so you can achieve your goals and chase your dreams. The amount of time that you spend on your distractions could be the amount of time that you spend on the actions responsible for achieving your goals. When you are consuming you are not thinking; what you are consuming is thinking for you. You only have a finite amount of decision-making power per day and you don't want to waste it. If you are consuming the wrong content then you are thinking unhelpful and irrelevant things. Is socialising with certain people useful to you? Is watching that TV program helping you in life? Truth is, it probably isn't. Instead, add that time to something which complements and aids your goals that way you can see yourself producing the life that you want. You are human and it is more than likely you will deviate from your path and lose your track every once in a while, which isn't a problem so long as the final destination doesn't change. As long as your core foundation remains solid and your principles are intact then you will always revert back to what is purposeful to you. One way to avoid losing track is through the creation of non-negotiable habits. Non-negotiable habits are habits that you stick to regardless of circumstance and situation. These habits could be getting eight hours of sleep every night, refraining from profanity or it could be anything that will be of benefit and significance to you and your development. Non-negotiable habits act as a pillar for you and build the fundamentals of your routine and if they aren't upheld then your whole system collapses. Merely, the thought of your system collapsing should send shivers down your spine because it'll leave you with no base, meaning there is nothing to build on, leaving you with a dream and not a reality.

Self-discipline is most easily achieved by focusing on you and limiting distractions. What concerns you, focus on; what doesn't concern you, leave it. In essence, quietly go about minding your own business. One way to rationalise the importance of discipline is through this analogy. Imagine there is a bank that credits your account each morning with £86,400. It carries over no balance from day-to-day. Every night the bank deletes whatever part of the balance you failed to use during the day. What would you do? Draw out every penny, right? Each of us has such a bank and its called time. Time credits you with 86,400 seconds every single day and every night it writes off as lost, whatever of this you have failed to invest to a good purpose is at your own risk and fault. Each day a new account is opened for you and each night burns the remains of the day. There is no drawing against tomorrow. You must live in the present on today's deposit. The clock is running so make the most of time as it is your most valuable asset. Every day you are given twenty-four hours which equals 1,440 minutes which equals 86,400 seconds; this time is non-refundable and non-renewable. Be selective of how you use your time on what activities and with which people. The way that I like to think of it is as an exchange or transaction. You are exchanging a portion of your life for whatever it may be; at work, it could be an hour of your life for £13 or it could be an hour of your life spent with a person whom you don't exactly gel with, ask yourself was that time invested wisely and was it worth it? Even if terms of your mood, if someone were to anger you due to what they said in ten seconds of speech, will you allow it to affect your whole day? The answer is no. Despite what's been said time doesn't actually exist. Time is an illusion. It is nothing but an agreed-upon construct. While time does have its uses we have been programmed to live our lives by this construct as if it is real. We have confused our shared construct with something that is tangible thus have become slaves to it. That's why it is cardinal to work according to your own schedule because what works for one may not work for another.

Now that you fathom the importance of time you understand the importance of how you should spend it and spend time effectively for that matter. You understand discipline is needed to help you learn to control your emotions and you can focus on building your life, career, and empire instead of throwing time away due to a lack of discipline. You don't want to work so hard for something just to go ruin what you got going for yourself. Know yourself well enough to avoid the people, places, and things that take you back to the habits that you worked so hard to break. You don't want to undo your progress as that's counter-intuitive.

Discipline can be tiring and as humans it is more than likely we will get lazy when it comes to completing the tasks that are required of us. However, discipline is what overpowers our feelings of laziness and is the reason why we don't make excuses for ourselves. Laziness and self-discipline don't go hand in hand because a man of discipline is a man who is planned, calculated and active. Laziness is natural but if we are to encounter sentiments of laziness then we should look to get up and get the relevant tasks over and done with because if we tell ourselves that we'll do it later we won't, because later never comes. I recommend that you first physically write out your ultimate goal, then break it down into smaller goals and assign deadlines to these small goals because it creates a sense of urgency that motivates you to accomplish them as you want to avoid disappointment. On a day-to-day basis, you should set out what you want to achieve as well, for the same reason- so that you can be optimally productive and so that you don't disappoint yourself. Some of us may be too lenient and forgiving on ourselves and if this is the case then we should seek out an accountability partner who could be a friend, family or anyone to be honest however it makes it better and more convenient if it is someone who is working towards a goal which is similar to yours. An accountability partner is someone who coaches you in terms of helping you keep to a commitment you've made. They check up to see if you're living up to your expectations and they will hold you responsible to the things you've said, and if you're not achieving what you need to achieve to the standard you should be achieving them to, then they should have the freedom to criticise you which should hopefully fill you with enough guilt not to disappoint again. It is recommended to create a regular schedule with them so you can frequently review your goals and adapt them if necessary and according to the progress you've made. An accountability partner is someone who is just double-checking to see if you've still got control over your life.

When it comes to control often the term gratification pops up and comes to mind. Gratification is the pleasure and satisfaction we gain from following our desires. Gratification is of two types: instant and delayed. Instant gratification is when you get what you want when you want, so there is no delay. Usually, instant gratification is an immediate and smaller reward that brings short-term pleasure. Delayed gratification is when someone resists the temptation of the immediate reward suppressing their whims and desires so they can go for the later reward which requires more patience. A person who tends to go for delayed gratification is a person of discipline, someone who can effectively self-regulate. People often indulge in activities that result in instant gratification as opposed to focusing on their future and looking at the bigger picture. Instead of networking, developing skills and learning they choose activities that will not benefit them in the future such as watching television, going partying, consuming themselves in social media and other meaningless nonsense. Developing a system where you can strike a balance between instant and delayed gratification is where you will find a sweet spot of current and future satisfaction. You will be able to live a lifestyle that you are content at the moment yet secure for the future.

Humans are people of ego and the development of discipline takes you on a journey teaching you not only patience but it humbles you through a series of failures. Humans are inadequate when it comes to gauging our ability. Everything that we know about ourselves is not as a result of our fore-thinking but rather it is a result of our past experiences, failures, and hindsight because these have tested us showing us our limitations. Prior to this, we strut in ego because we often overestimate ourselves and look to push our capacity beyond what is possible for us at that moment in time. This can explain why someone may enter a relationship despite seeing apparent red flags; the person believes that they hold the capacity to change the other person even if the other person doesn't have the desire to change. After facing failure you then return to a point of humbleness because we weren't as clever and patient as you anticipated and then the cycle repeats. Discipline requires you to stick to your plan and suppress your desires. Desires lead to sudden urges causing you to act in ways you normally wouldn't but you would surely look stupid compromising your self-respect and progress to satisfy our desires. We love making excuses for ourselves especially when we shouldn't. When you begin justifying something you will continue doing it because you see nothing wrong with it. You become desensitised to the habit that you have created in a way. You may do something telling yourself that it will only be one-off occurrence only for it to happen again, again and again, but what happens is alarm bells don't ring or if they do you suppress your thoughts and lie to yourself, making excuses and justify why you are doing it. This principle can also be applied to when we are not doing something. We could have built a good habit which we maintained on a consistent basis but then an event may arise that is out of our control throwing us off the course of action which leads to a disruption in our routine. Instead of re-establishing the routine we are creating reasons as to why that good habit isn't that beneficial and how you can better spend your time when all you are actually doing is making excuses so you don't have to endure the temporary hardships associated with that good habit.

A huge part of self-discipline is disciplining yourself so that you can focus and create a tunnel vision so you can effectively achieve your goal whatever it may be. It is far easier to stick to something and maintain something if you have love and passion for it otherwise it can seem a drag and you may be unwilling to do it especially in times where you lack motivation and drive. That's why it is crucial to do things with purpose and passion so set your goals with that in mind. When setting your goal, begin with the end in mind. You don't want to waste your energy chasing something which is not of value. Everyone wants one thing ultimately which is freedom because freedom means time which can be spent however one pleases and time spent correctly can render a feeling of fulfillment. You want to set a goal that is in line with your passion that way the reward isn't diminishing and so that work never really feels like a chore. When you have been around money, money doesn't impress you. When you've been partying, that gets old. If you are subject to a particular lifestyle of thing in your life it diminishes in value over time so chasing the illusions that others are after proves rather futile so it is of better benefit utilising your energy properly. A way to maintain discipline is through awareness. Measure the utility of your actions when on the pursuit of your goals. Weighing up the pros and cons with a cost-benefit analysis allows you to see why you are doing what you are doing and what is the ultimate reward. Use your past and people around you as a motivation even if they aren't supportive. Often our environments can condition us into who we are today. You don't need to look up to anyone growing up; you can just have people you don't want to be like. That can be used as motivation to keep away from the bad actions of the people in your environment and a reason to strive and achieve different levels of success which may be unusual or unheard of in your community.

Fear

A comfort zone is a place of familiarity, ease, and relief. In the comfort zone, you can relax since you will have low levels of stress, anxiety and other negative energies. Anyone who is living in their comfort zone is a person who may make progress but is most definitely someone who is hitting targets way beneath the standard they should be setting for themselves and they are someone who is working below their capacity. The comfort zone is where minimal effort is applied and barely acceptable results are returned. The comfort zone is subjective to each individual so one person's comfort zone could be another person's hell on earth because they are on different levels at different capacities. Everyone will eventually enter a comfort zone but it shouldn't be a place they look to settle especially if they have a growth mindset. Stepping out of your comfort zone allows you to test your abilities under stress and pressure which builds you stronger for the next time your skills are required; it allows you to challenge yourself which can help you perform at your peak.

You are most likely in your comfort zone right now in a place of low stress, little challenge and poorer levels of self-education which is deleterious on your personal growth. In the comfort zone you feel safe and in control because you are in an environment you are accustomed to, you can accurately assess risk and consequence hence you are hardly threatened but once you decide to try something new which will elevate you to the next level then you will have to look to leave your comfort zone. It is far better you make the choice to leave your comfort zone and develop compared to being forced out of it having to deal with the spontaneity of a circumstance. As a person leaves the comfort zone they enter the fear zone which is the place the vast majority quit, retracting back to the warmth of their comfort zone because this transition gets too hard and too much for them. The fear zone is space of doubt and confusion where a person's lack of confidence begins to show because they come across the opinions of others which leads them to start finding excuses as to why they couldn't expand out of their comfort zone. If a person was strong enough to overcome their doubts and conquer their fear then they would progress into the learning zone where they actually address the challenges and problems that need to be addressed to develop. Through this, they acquire new skills. After this point, they are experiencing growth and have extended their comfort zone. In the growth zone, they have achieved the objectives they originally set out to achieve and look to set new goals. Discernibly with time, your growth zone becomes your comfort zone because you have familiarised yourself with it and then the cycle repeats. Throughout your life you will continuously be at one of these four stages: comfort, fear, learning or growth no matter how successful you are or how many accolades you have to your name.

Fear is a primal emotion and it has both a psychological and emotional response. Fear is caused by the threat of danger, pain or harm however these factors are not just in relation to the protection and preservation of our lives as a survival tactic but also when we choose to enter new territories and try new things. The thing about being in fear is that we perceive danger because we don't know of the consequences or outcome of what will happen but the truth is we may over-exaggerated these fears and create irrational ideas in our minds as to why we can't do things and explore new options. Fear is a prowling force that can rob you of joy, confidence and hope nevertheless it is completely normal and everyone experiences at different levels and magnitudes but you can't allow fear to control you otherwise you will live a life of no risk and no reward. You will at heart and in mind be nothing but a prisoner and victim of your own fear, constantly in a state of worry. Worrying is a waste of time. It doesn't change anything. In fact, it messes with your mind and steals your happiness. You must challenge your fears otherwise you are held back from achieving greatness because of fear imprisoning you, trapping you in a bubble due to the fact you are afraid of what people will say or think of you or the overshadowing possibility of failure. Fear is created because a result has been created before the performance has been conducted. This result isn't known for certain but since the person has told themselves what they think will be the outcome they prepare themselves for that exact outcome. A public speaker's first time speaking on a large platform may fear that they freeze up, lose their words or the crowd will not receive them well. However, this speaker has never attempted to do a speech on such a large stage before so how could they possibly determine what will happen? You don't know what will happen unless you give it a go for yourself or have seen others give it a go otherwise that thing will forever remain a void of possibility and chance.

Fear causes doubt and doubt is a feeling of uncertainty or a lack of conviction. Doubt leads to confusion and loss of belief and it all stems from one thing- a lack of self-confidence. Doubt is fine and in fact, it is desirable because in reasonable doses it can be healthy when it comes to introspection and self-judgement. Doubt shouldn't be something which is preventative but rather something which encourages the re-thinking of a situation or action, giving you a sharper insight. Fear is the element that is responsible for a man's actions. Everyone experiences fear in different ways and if a person can't conquer it then they will live a life below their potential. A person who lives in fear is often a person who knows no better so show compassion, sympathy, and love towards them so they can truly realise their potential especially if they can't see their gift. Sometimes it is not even about realising their potential but a person may have had a life of difficulty and struggle and hence their experiences have shaped them and their minds have been conditioned into thinking a certain way when certain situations happen so you must understand someone's actions towards you may have nothing to do with you. Their identity is centred around the trauma they've experienced. They have no idea who they are outside of this trauma and are afraid of becoming victims again and that fear terrifies them.

One reason why people fear is because they don't want to face a harsh reality or more specifically rejection. I remember as a child my dad used to take me to the local recreational ground and as I grew older I developed, at the time, a passion for football. I used to see kids playing football in little groups at the park and always wanted to join in but I was always too scared. My dad would always encourage me to go to them and ask if I could join in but I never would. Looking back in hindsight it was because I was afraid of rejection and being told no. I remember I would try and reason with myself telling myself that I can't play because those other kids seem better than me or they were older than me or whatever excuse I could make up. Had I been that age with the knowledge that I have now then I would've taken the risk because the reward is quite great at the time and the risk was super low or if it wasn't low it was made high due to self-imposed limitations and beliefs I placed on myself and in my mind. What was the worst that could happen? Truth is not much really. The worst thing is they could tell me was "no" but then it is what it is and I could try my luck elsewhere and the best-case scenario is they say yes and I play football with them having an enjoyable and memorable time perhaps even walking away with a bunch of new friends. Whichever way I could flip it, in that circumstance, I wasn't going to die or have my life threatened by being rejected so rejection really didn't matter.

Fear is something everyone has or will experience and this is because everyone faces uncertainty which could expose their vulnerabilities. An entrepreneur may confront fears every time they come up with a new idea. They feel fear from the doubt that this new venture may not work, they have doubts in their own ability to manifest it and they fear because they don't know how they will go about something so big. Everyone may not be an entrepreneur but everyone is a CEO. A CEO is in charge of key managerial decisions and everyone has a responsibility and is the CEO of their own life. They choose to promote, terminate and delegate people and tasks where necessary for their best interest. People that have your best interest at heart are people who can help facilitate your vision. Stop letting your ideas and talent go to waste due to doubt and a lack of confidence. Someone with less ability will surpass you simply because they believe in themselves more. The best way to overcome fear and doubt is through an entrepreneurial mindset even if you aren't an entrepreneur. Think of it by projecting yourself at an old age say seventy years old with health problems and low energy levels. You want to have minimised the number of regrets that you have and the regret, in this case, is paths not taken; you will be haunted on what would have happened and could have happened. You don't want to sit in contemplation on your death bed cataloguing your regrets. It becomes obvious to you once you hit old age, that you wouldn't regret trying something and failing because you didn't pass up on the opportunity as it was once in a lifetime.

Take risks it's the best thing you can do for yourself because if you win then you see success and if you fail you learn a lesson and gain some wisdom. One reason why people fear is because they are too worried about being judged and the thoughts other people will have of them. Do not allow people to project their fear on to you. People will doubt you and question your ideas. You may present an idea to someone and they may argue you with you telling you why you can't do such a thing. Not everyone will see your vision and understand you. For instance, you may choose to take on a business venture where you make the decision to leave your job and people may tell you "you won't be able to pay for rent" or "you won't be able to provide for yourself" or "it might fail and you'll be left unemployed." If you take a look at the list of billionaires and read their stories you come to find that a lot of their stories share similarities in the sense that they all faced pressure from others or negative judgement from others which inflicted them with some level of doubt and even during the process of building their empire they would often face difficulties which made them question whether it was all worth it. Regardless, they all persevered despite occasions where their vision was cloudy. They believed in themselves, the value they brought to the table and the strength of the idea they had to offer. If you live your life based on what someone else's opinion then are you really living your life or are you allowing them to take control over you and make you a victim and another robotic vessel who follows the system of the majority. Don't sell yourself out because it is what everyone else is doing and don't care too much about the criticism unless it is constructive.

A person who fears too much is someone who is too cautious and often a negative thinking person, always expecting and predicting the worst from a person or situation. This type of person is vulnerable and due to their negative mentality, they consequentially live a life of negative reality. Vulnerable people perhaps weren't always vulnerable but due to their prior experiences they have their guard up to protect themselves which is okay but it becomes a problem when your guard is too defensive that you can't take risks or partake in certain activities because you expect something to happen. All being vulnerable does, and this is especially the case when your vulnerability is a choice, is you're made weak. Often cases, when you are vulnerable, people act in peculiar ways. Personally, I know this because I have played mind games with the people around me. I have acted confused, weak and dumb to see how those around me will act and move. In reality, I am paying attention to their behaviour when they don't think I am. People like to prey on your weaknesses using it as an opportunity to take advantage of you, manipulating you to get what they want. They take your kindness for weakness. This initial fear that you created within yourself as a turtle-shell defence proves useless because in the end you still will get used and manipulated or you will be left lonely and unsuccessful. Don't be too worried, take risks and have faith but don't be foolish when doing so, remain diligent. Expect the best, plan for the best but be prepared for surprises.

Regret

You can't run from a storm forever. You have got to learn to stand up to it. There is dignity in surviving a storm. You will never walk out of a storm the same person that went in. Storms cause pain which manifests into regret.

Regret is a poison that only gets more lethal over time and it's easier said than done but don't give yourself anything to regret. It, just like fear, is an emotion that is completely normal and something that everyone experiences and this is due to the fact things are done rashly or not done at all. Regret doesn't come alone; it packages itself with other negative emotions such as guilt, disappointment, and frustration which spur on the initial feelings of regret. You may have done favours when you had no room to do them for people. You may have done things that put you in a hole for a while just to see others smile! You may have taken worries off people's backs and added them to yours. You may have proved your loyalty and true friendship to others on numerous occasions yet still see yourself faced against those who you've helped in battle and rivalry. You may have fed mouths that have talked down and gossiped about you. You may have wiped the tears off the faces of people that have caused yours. You may have picked up people that have tried to knock you down. You may have done favours for people that could do nothing for you. You may have been there for people that have not been there for you. Regret is something that needs to be tackled either alone or with someone you trust. It is important to decide who you share your pain with, if you decide to do so, because information in the hands of the wrong people can lead to further pain and regret. We all have the feeling of regret when you tell another person too much; people are often temporary and may not be your friends in the future. However if you do mistakenly tell the wrong person too much or anything at all, ironic as it is, have no regrets for doing so because it the end it was a life lesson which made you wiser for the next time and it is their loss of a friend due to their disloyalty and selfishness. Do not regret a single one of those actions because you need to refuse losing yourself in the hatred of others. You must continue to be you because you are who you are and it is in your nature to be considerate and caring. Life isn't easy and it never will be but through all of that, you should do what's in your best ability to help others. Regret isn't only about people but can also be about situations, yet the same principle still applies and you should never regret a day in your life:

good days bring happiness, bad days give experiences, your worst days teach lessons and your best days bring memories.

Regret is either short-term or long-term. Short-term regret is when dealing with minuscule things which may seem significant at the time but in reality aren't when looking back at it in retrospection. Long-term regret, on the other hand, is when dealing with something that has and will affect you over a larger duration of time. When it comes to overcoming feelings of regret, especially short-term regret, one tactic that can be used in order to maintain a resilient and strong mental state is applying the 'five by five rule' which is where you spend no longer than five minutes upset about something which isn't going to be relevant or worth your attention in five years' time. Every time you get upset at something or someone, ask yourself if you were to die tomorrow, was it worth your time being angry? We get emotional over the tiniest things which hold little to no significance. Just because we dedicated time and effort into someone or something and we didn't achieve what we wanted to achieve it doesn't mean we have to dwell over it. However, we need to be in control of our emotions because emotions have an effect on the way we act. The worst thing we can do is react to a situation without analysing it because making permanent decisions over temporary emotions can be devastating. One example I've seen is when someone decides to get a tattoo of the person they are dating. A person may make you feel happy, loved and cared for at that moment in time but after that moment has passed and differences appear between the two of you and the relationship is deemed incompatible then you are left with a permanent tattoo which every time you see fills you with instant regret and thoughts of a distant memory.

Pain and hurt are amplified by regret. Regret is either from taking accountability and blame for factors out of your control or from you seeking repentance for your actions which may have caused damage to someone else. Regardless of the reason for regret, the want remains the same- which is to reverse the damage done and the pain caused to others but that is not an option as time is something we have no control over. True pain is when you're put in a situation that no amount of money can fix. One circumstance that this was especially true of this is the story of my Uncle H and my grandfather. My uncle was incarcerated for some of crime so his parents were left to their own devices for the most part, but of course, my father and his other brother and sister helped out and we visited my grandparents every weekend as per usual. However, two years into my uncle's sentence, my grandfather who was a very active man even at his age of seventy-some years experienced a stroke causing him to lose control of his body leading to his collapse and on-impact with the ground he passed. My grandfather was on his way towards Friday prayer when this happened. What everybody was shocked about was the fact this incident happened so unexpectedly; it wasn't as if he was lying in a hospital bed slowly waiting on the angel of death. The mood of everyone was glum for obvious reasons. Everybody was mourning. My Uncle H learned about his father's death on a phone call whilst in jail. I think there were two things that hurt him the most. The first not being able to see his father for the last time; it hurts him to think that his father's last memory of their youngest son is one behind bars instead of something more positive and uplifting. The other thing is not being able to physically be there for his mother and provide her with the emotional support she needed whilst dealing with the loss of life. Fortunately for my Uncle H, he could effectively deal with the pain and sorrow due to his 'it is what it is' mentality where he had come to accept the reality of life and that things do happen out of his control. I am sure, to this day, he still has feelings of regret creeping into his mind but he can effectively suppress these thoughts and use his energy to engage with more positive thoughts and opportunities.

Regret develops into dwelling on what could have been. We start to look in hindsight and see what we could've done if certain variables were changed or if we did one thing instead of another. Regret takes away from our purpose and anything that takes us away from our ultimate goals is nothing but a distraction. Distractions cause us to steer away from achieving our objectives and hitting targets. We may find due to dwelling we lose momentum on our road to success. We need to rediscover what we were originally attempting to achieve and once that ultimate goal is set, we need to break it down into small short-term targets. By doing this we have direction and direction is far more important than speed. We can be achieving a lot, and a lot in a short period of time but it is useless if we are achieving that which doesn't benefit us or is a part of our plan. One thing that can be done to prevent the proliferation of regret is by having respect for you because if you don't respect yourself, you would be naïve to believe others will respect you, your goals or your targets. In a way, self-respect cuts your losses short because it means you have set boundaries for your own protection.

Dwelling is when you choose to linger over something that has already happened and it is most likely something which is a source of your unhappiness. Dwelling is the bitter aftertaste of regret. Dwelling on a situation downloads it into your memory and your subconscious and it will cause the situation to continuously revisit you which exposes you to a risk of not fulfilling your goals or objectives as these negative events are on repeat in your head. Dwelling is the number one enemy of progress. Obsessing over the highs and lows of life causes you to fluctuate between moments of ecstasy and despair which could result in you turning to things such as drugs and alcohol to suppress your true emotions and numb your pain. Disguising your pain or looking for quick fixes will not help you; it is better for you to identify the issues and look to see how you can fix that. If it is pain caused through something out of your control then you have to strengthen your mind and remember that the world will carry on spinning regardless of your situation. Don't feel a need to dwell on the past and don't feel sorry for yourself. Whatever has happened has happened to you and it doesn't define you and it is just a phase in life that you are going through. What better defines you is how you carry yourself and find solutions when in times of difficulty and hardship. You shouldn't let anything in your past affect you from moving forward anyway since you can't do anything about the past. People worry about what is now instead of what is next. Fixating on present problems does no good for us unless we are working on a solution; the future is bright and holds so much potential so it would make more sense to work on that. There will always be another opportunity because time goes on but then again time doesn't stop for anybody. When we experience times of sadness, pain or trauma we have a choice when it comes to our response to it. We can tell ourselves a certain story and re-run it time and time again which will eventually let it affect our future. A single event can prevent you from progress and achieving the future we so eagerly seek. Take ownership of the situation, accept it, learn from it and move on with more strength and wisdom than before and if you can embrace the situation because it will make the burden you hold lesser.

Sometimes in life, things don't go the way you want or you do something wrong and there's nothing you can do about it. Just put it in the past and move forward. Losses with the exclusion of death generally tend to be temporary anyways a business person can have a losing day but a profitable week. They can have a losing week but a profitable month. You can have a losing month but a profitable year. Playing the long game well gives you not only success but builds character. Loss in regards to death is a reminder that nothing in this life is permanent. You can have someone one with you one minute and they could be gone the next. Don't dwell on things you can't fix but if it is a singular event that throws your mood off then perhaps you can try and prepare for it so when the time comes you won't be affected as badly as you could be. Life is so ironic, it takes sadness to know what happiness is, noise to appreciate silence and absence to value presence. Some emotions can't be truly experienced unless a person has been without it or experienced the opposite of it. You can't appreciate winning if you've never lost, you can't appreciate love if you've never been hated. These experiences help us conceptualise the notion of value. Value is determined by our ability to do with or without something or someone. If you can do without something it is of lower value than you have assigned to it and therefore not a necessity meaning you can do without it.

Critics & Labels

On your journey of self-development, you will cross paths with negative people and energies. It is weird how when you are on route to achieving something remarkable people take a sudden interest in your business, they seem concerned about you and engaged in your affairs. You may be fooled into thinking that this is genuine care, which it could be, but you may find that it isn't that and they aren't worried about how or what you are doing; they're concerned about how or what you're doing compared to them. You will have to learn how to respond correctly to them so that you aren't side-lined off of your path and destination. People will always have an opinion and something to say about what another person is doing or how they're living their life. People will sit back and piece together everything about everybody's life but their own. Humans love to criticise each other and hate because hating is free and because the haters are often living a painful, miserable and dim life. There is no medicine for hate meaning you can't reason with someone who's filled with jealousy and envy because these people can only see their cause and no one else's which blinds their judgement. You can't mention hard-core proof to them.

No amount of statistics or research evidence will be enough for them. They can't face the facts. Those who are against you love to cause confusion. No matter how much you clarify things, they will never be satisfied as the truth will offend them. So be it. Don't look for the approval of others. Rarely will you be hated by someone doing more than you but it is always the people that have nothing going for them that waste their time hating on others. Usually, those who criticise you and are doing more than you give constructive criticism, provide guidance for you and give you improvement prompts whilst those doing less just contribute toxic energy of no real substance. It is easy to entertain a hater and try to prove yourself to them but as a wise man once said: "never argue with a fool because people can't tell which one is which from a distance."

The employment of self-control teaches you how to conduct yourself in times where you feel the urge to be petty or disrespectful. You can't change the behaviour of others. Some people are just stuck in their ways. When people act shady, allow them. When people betray your trust, allow them. However, you should never be petty and sink to their level. You need to understand that their choices are a direct reflection of who they are and not who you are. Bitterness does no good for you.

Criticism only has an effect if you allow it to. Everybody has a mouth but not every voice counts. Pay no mind to every criticism you undergo; the hatred you undergo and are subject to as it is a waste of energy responding to everything that is directed to you. Other's opinions affect us because we want to feel accepted. Learn to discipline your emotions because if you don't your enemies will use them against you. The ability to bounce back and move on is a skill so we should develop resilience. Remember the moon doesn't lose any of its beauty in the night sky even if there's a dog barking at it, it remains unaffected. Everybody wants to talk about how they would do this and that in your position. For example, the rich in society are often subject to fierce scrutiny by those who aren't as rich as them especially in regard to their spending habits. People would say things along the lines of "why don't they donate more to charity?" or "why do they choose to spend their money on that, what a waste!" but when you compare the two people alongside each other you find that the rich and the not so rich are similar proportionally or that the rich do more in charitable and commendable acts than their less wealthy counterparts.

You can avoid a lot of the drama that others bring by keeping quiet. Privacy is power because what people don't know, people can't ruin. There is beauty in privacy because when you don't tell your plans to others your plans don't get messed up. Unless they have a genuine love for you or words of encouragement don't you share your ideas as their negative minds will offer negative inputs telling you why your plan won't work. Your voice is what matters most, not others. Don't sabotage yourself by letting other people determine how important you are or how successful your vision will be. Humans can only see as far as their limitations and are often short-sighted. People try to tell you that "that won't happen," or "it is not realistic," or "you don't have what it takes." All they are doing is exclaiming their reality at that moment in time, not yours. Another reason why privacy can help us is because it teaches us to have control over our situation and avoids us from looking the fool. No one knows how hard you work, how many hours you put in behind the scenes; so rely on yourself for approval, not the outside world. Don't be foolish and expose every blessing or new idea in your life to everyone and think that they'd be happy for you. Some will be but many won't. Learn to keep things private and not to share too much with those who could possibly harm you. Very private people have mastered the art of telling you little about themselves but doing it in such a way you think you know a lot. Privacy is essential because if you are to tell someone your plans and what you are about to do you expose yourself to risk and vulnerability. They may hate on you and you may never know it because it may never be made obvious. Don't take it for granted that you helped someone that they will care for you and help and support your cause because they might not see themselves as someone who owes you loyalty despite what you think.

In life, you will come across a lot of people who hold the image of success and stability but the truth is nobody has it figured it. When pursuing what you want the only thing that separates the winners and the losers is when it comes to quitting. Winners never quit. Yes, you may experience every emotion there is on your journey but importantly is you see your journey through. Don't believe anyone who says that they have it all together; there's no such thing. Every single one of us is fighting an unseen battle that may be disguised by a brave and strong exterior but a battle nonetheless hence why compassion is so vital. Put yourself in the shoes of someone else. Those who portray a lifestyle where they having everything figured out are fake and are doing all of that because they think it will boost their status and social perception. These people love to give advice and talk about making it to their level but their level doesn't exist, they are dream sellers and are selling you an illusion. Also, beware of people with excessive advice or ridicule but no results to back them. Their words of wisdom either aren't working for them or they aren't applying it to their own life. The blind can't lead the blind and not everyone can get you to where you're destined to go in life.

People always like to drop their two cents in what doesn't concern them. The first thing that you should look for in those who offer you help is have they done it for themselves. If they haven't done it themselves then you're taking advice which is theoretical, they are not giving you data from experience. Think about the person you're taking advice from. Have they ever been in your position to be giving you advice or has someone close to them been in a similar situation? A lot of people aren't qualified to be giving advice because they have no experience to back what they are saying. Some people take more interest in trying to solve other people's problems than their own. People can talk about how to have successful marriage but do they have a successful one themselves? They can tell you how to get rich by investing your money but they haven't tried it for themselves? They may tell you how to raise your kids without having any experience with kids in their life. These people don't understand some things are easier said than done. These people may be informative but are far from knowledgeable. If life worked how it does in theory then a lot of problems wouldn't exist. In fact, there is this ancient story wherein a far Middle-Eastern land there was an ongoing conflict. There was this one student who went through the schooling and military academy, this student was top of his class. He was able to know all the theory of war and learned all the war tactics. After his schooling and training, he was called up to join the battlefield. The student brought all of his books relating to war. The general questioned him as to why he brought all of this content relating to war with him and the student replied because he believed it would be useful in understanding the enemy. The general instructed the student to leave behind all his books because on the battlefield the war isn't won with information but rather knowledge and wisdom because in war battles are fought with emotion which books cannot teach.

When following your heart to turn your dreams into reality, you need to remain in control. You will need to delegate tasks to others but the overall project will have to be in charge by you because you know what you want, how you want it done and to what standard. Yes, others will try and advise you and you can choose to listen to them and take their advice on board however you must remain true to your intentions and make sure you are not compromising your dream to fulfil someone else's. We need to take responsibility for what we do by grabbing the bull by its horns. When making a choice make sure those choices aren't based solely off of the opinions others have voiced. Y are your own person and what worked for them may not work for you, there is no recipe for success so you may not be able to replicate another person's success because times change and things develop. However, what you can do it extract lessons from their journey especially lessons they learned in their hardship and try to build your character to be resilient as theirs was. Listen to everybody but you don't need to implement every piece of advice they give just elements perhaps until you found a system that works for you. You should have a level of self-love and appreciation of your worth that you detach yourself from negative energies and surround yourself with realism and positivity. Let your optimism produce the type of energy that effects change in the world around you and don't be affected by the change in the world around you. Don't allow people to come into your space and let their negativity change your outlook on the world but let your light shine so bright it forces their outlook to change. That being said some energy is too negative you're better off avoiding them. When you associate with those you always have to explain yourself to, you'll inevitably end up unsuccessful. Nothing will please their ears and you can't build with them. These people are jealous and don't be naïve because jealousy isn't always about what you have in a materialistic sense but people may envy how others have loved you; how others show love to you and have love for you. People envy the way you might have handled a situation that they might have struggled over. What they thought would have broken you. Some people envy your intelligence and how you can take action to make things happen. They envy you because something they couldn't get past you breezed through with ease. However, don't be quick to assume the role of a victim when it comes to labels and criticism. Some people may have your best interests at heart but have a different, harsher and stricter way of showing it. Learn to appreciate those who are valuable in your life. If somebody is always on to you about doing better, keep them around because they do not hate on you or talk down on you they just see the potential in you and want you to see and realise your worth.

A negative person will always have a problem for every solution. Some people's brains aren't programmed the same way as yours they will point out a hundred reasons why something might not work but they'll never point out the hundreds of reasons why it might work. Follow your path, work hard and have faith. Keep away from those people who belittle your ambitions. Sometimes you come across individuals who underplay your success and accomplishment. There are three situations in regard to this matter: they undermine, discredit or disregard your achievement. They undermine your achievement by downplaying its importance or the value of the achievement through comparison. They also try discrediting your achievement claiming the success of it didn't come from you or your hard work. Another thing they do is disregard the achievement by not acknowledging it whatsoever.

Avoid putting yourself in places and positions where there is an opportunity for people to critique you condescendingly or assign labels to you. Don't let anyone put you in a box. People like to define you by your mistakes because it makes them feel more secure knowing that, in their eyes, you will always be better than them and you will always surpass them in the different things of life. The problem with being labelled is that you might actually be convinced and believe that you deserve to be in that box. The effect this has is that you may sabotage every opportunity for happiness and success because you have started to believe you are unworthy and undeserving of that happiness and success. You begin to believe that due to the mistakes you've made that and then have been exaggerated by others has created you in a person who has a tendency to create self-imposed limitations. These limitations may be so subtle or something so obvious but ingrained in culture such as benchmarks we set for ourselves. We need to stop arbitrary assigning certain benchmarks to specific ages. This only leads to making poor decisions or a constant feeling that you need to keep up. Everyone works at their own pace hence why two people from the same age group may be at two different places in life, one may be single whilst the other a grandparent. When someone tries to keep up they don't think rationally and this can unleash a toxic competitive spirit in them. Success is commonly defined by material objects whether it be the German car, Swiss watch piece or Italian designer clothes; trying to match other people can lead to poor financial decisions which leave you under even more stress. It is better to live within your means as opposed to living extravagantly trying to match people whose approval you look for. If we don't follow these benchmarks we find ourselves alienated in society because we find that these labels define who we are and without them we are nothing. Labelling people is dangerous. We are conditioned to judge people based on their looks, behaviour, job and the list goes on. It happens subconsciously even if we don't have ill intent. Labels can limit others and limit your interactions with them. Even labels with good intentions can create resentment and animosity because the person who you've labelled may now feel as though they have to live up to a certain expectation and they now feel a burden and pressure that wasn't previously there.

When you go through a rough patch in your life you may find yourself put in a box by society bound by its expectations. Society has a tendency to associate certain occasions with certain consequences so when you break past that mould and don't fit the model then it is a surprise and concern to everyone. They may come up with statements questioning your happiness or the reasons for your happiness because that happiness isn't often associated with a person who has been through what you have been through. A feeling of "who are you to be happy?" circulates. They expect you to disappear off the face of the Earth instead of getting back involved in the community and its functions. People may peg you with certain labels and expect you to be restricted by these labels. People have feelings of animosity towards you because you were meant to stay in that box. Stand up for yourself and your beliefs because if you accept manipulation you will be conforming to their opinion of you and continue taking these advantages as they will view themselves as superior. People love to put others in a box anchoring them to the mistake they've made. One reason why they do this is that it is an excuse for them to focus their energy on you rather than their own mistakes and shortcomings. You need to remember an event in your life is only one chapter of the book. A book has a number of chapters so you can't allow yourself to be defined by that one specific event. You can't allow people to label you and restrict you in a psychological box and think that is all your self-worth means.

Putting people in a box could also mean holding people to unrealistic expectations even if they are in a positive way. Putting a person on a pedestal is the worst place to put them because they have no room to error. One of the main reasons this happens is because of a person's past experience with someone who may share some similarities and characteristics even if you're yet to do something wrong or behaved in a way that is considered wrong in their eyes. In the past, a person may have tolerated negative behaviour and the consequences of this behaviour but eventually, they leave and move on yet still carrying these negative stereotypes with them. When a mistake is made by this new person they get painted with the same brush as the previous person they've encountered and all the previous person's errors have been displaced onto the new person. This behaviour is due to the displacement of negative energy and emotion on someone else. One example is when a female has spent time in a toxic relationship where she was disrespected, used and abused. When a person is good but makes one mistake they are quickly labelled titles such as a hypocrite and become subject to criticism from all angles. You should promote positivity and this is because if you treat a person for how they are they will become worse but if you treat a person for how they could be you promote them to become who they should be. You shouldn't ever underestimate the impact of your words and support whether small or big.

Prejudice

Thinking is a critical part of mental processing. On one end of the spectrum you have overthinking which leads to stress and anxiety and on the other end you have under-thinking which results in assumptions being made that could potentially hurt your social life or even your career and business. Assumptions are made all the time and without realising because it is so easy to make them especially if you don't have time to think something through or analyse a situation thoroughly. Assumptions can lock us off from possibilities as well as limit our perspective. It doesn't allow us to see the raw truth for what it is. You can become a victim of assumption making very easily so to avoid this you should base your judgement based on known facts. The lack of thinking leads to assumptions and assumptions are the cause of prejudice. Prejudice is a preconceived opinion that is not based on reason or actual experience and they can be either positive or negative preconceptions. We become prejudice when we lack knowledge of a situation or person which leads us to make unfair and unreasonable judgements. Holding prejudice thoughts is a character flaw. Character flaws need to be dealt with as they can manifest into toxic traits. One method which helps to fix any character flaw is looking at it how it affects the people that you love. When you see the people you dearly love affected by your character flaws in a negative way it hurts you seeing them hurt. You may find yourself hurting them to such an extent you surpass a point of forgiveness and a relationship is ruined.

Prejudice stems from traditional and culture views. People are conditioned to believe certain things from a young age. They are taught to assign labels, hold stigmas against and put connotations on different things. This has meant things such as how you carry yourself, how you conduct yourself and how you dress plays a huge role in how others deal with you despite however much we deny it but if you stand on values and principles most people will respect you. A person dressed in uniform is more likely to be seen as dominant and authoritative compared to someone dressed in cargo shorts and a polo t-shirt simply because our brains have been conditioned into believing stereotypes so certain things are viewed as powerful, influential and superior despite us not having scratched the surface delving deeper into the personality of a person. A couple who decide to go out on a date to a Michelin star restaurant with their three-year-old child who acts uncontrollably throwing peas at fellow diners and has a tendency to throw fits will be received negatively with the parents being coined as incapable and negligent despite the fault not being theirs directly. The parents are received in this way because of social norms and expectations when dining at a restaurant of that sort even though the child's behaviour is completely normal for their age. This is because society has drilled thoughts into us telling us that we must act in a certain way at certain places. This can be observed across different facets of life from domestic to business life. If a person was to attend a business meeting in a tracksuit whilst the room is filled with executives dressed in expensive Italian suits others will question the person and their seriousness because the person is deemed unprofessional as they do not meet the social norm.

You will find that integral prejudice starts off with something which only affects you but this in due course develops into displays of disrespect towards others. You should never walk around with preconceived thoughts about another person. You should suspect evil of no one until you see for yourself how a person is. Humans have a bias to the first source they hear from and tend to adopt the beliefs of what the initially hear. For instance, if you overheard someone talking about a certain sport team and how well they play then you are naturally inclined to believe that the sports team is in fact good so when the topic of sports comes up in a conversation you will most likely talk about the sports team in a good light despite having no knowledge of your own about the sports team. The same way you shouldn't judge a book by its cover and should turn the pages to reveal its content; you should really judge a person on what's internal so their character and personality, not external factors or information from secondary sources. You should never disrespect anyone or underestimate them, being prejudice is disrespectful. You need to respect yourself and respect those around you because tables can turn and situations change so although someone may be deemed inferior now, it could be the case, in the future they may be seen as someone powerful, respected and highly valued. You should get to know a person for them and this should be done for you because once you familiarise yourself with a person you are less likely to make prejudgements.

Prejudice can also develop into feelings of jealousy and envy. Jealousy and envy are elicited from hate. Hate is a strong emotion and feeling of intense dislike for someone or something. Hating others is like drinking poison and waiting for the other person to die. Hate damages you and your mental well-being so holding grudges and negative thoughts against and about others won't make them feel guilty or hurt but it will make you pessimistic and depressed. Someone may seem like they have everything there is to have as if the world was in their favour but in reality, you don't know about the trials and tribulations that that person had to undergo and endure or the sacrifices they had to make. We, as humans, are making judgements based on what is on the external, which is wrong. We know nothing except what is apparent and on the surface level but when it comes to the deeper matters; matters that are beyond the physical realm we have no knowledge about. How can you have envy towards someone? You haven't the slightest clue what that person's journey was like, especially if the person achieved something such as financial success. You don't know how many long nights, early mornings, broke days, empty refrigerators, bus journeys, overdrafts, negative account balances, saver menus and all the other things they had to experience and go through. It can almost be guaranteed they faced so many "no's" and rejections on their journey and they would have found life tough. They may have even shed tears during the process but despite all of that they achieved what they set out to achieve.

Prejudice may lead to disrespect directed towards others. Not everyone will be as privileged as you maybe and this is the reason why you shouldn't act in a way that is too prideful and boasts. You should never knock another man's hard work and hustle because you never know another person's situation. Each individual is responsible for their own situation and their hustle may be necessary for them to feed their family and pay their bills. It is best that you mind your own business and if you cross paths with someone who could do with some help then try help and facilitate them instead of judge and discriminate against them. Some people will check up on you to see how you're doing not because they care but so they can stay in the loop of your personal business. The answers that you give them will help them determine how much respect they should give to you because these people are so ego-driven. They will ask you questions beginning with "do you still...?" because they are in the hope that you aren't making progress because they want to hold what they think is superiority over you. If they genuinely cared about you they would ask about how you're doing and feeling conversing about plans for the future. Don't be stupid enough to think they care simply because they are asking questions about you. A true, authentic conversation requires a balanced exchange of information so the volume and significance of the information that you tell them, they should ideally reciprocate and feed similar back. Prejudice can happen even after you have met someone. You are constantly learning new things about others and you may judge a person based on old and dated information they've told you on a previous occasion. The problem with judging a person is that when you're constantly making assumptions about them meaning you damage your capacity to relate to them on an unbiased level. You are always assuming you know what they think and feel; so as opposed to listening and communicating you assume you understand what is being said and what they mean but in fact, it is a preconception fuelled by your forward-thinking. This means when someone is in a predicament facing adversity you assume you can help the person based on how they previously dealt with things however by doing this you forget to look at the essence of a problem meaning that the problem is not effectively resolved and dealt with. You never know what the next soul is going through, what hardships they've had to endure. Everyone handles situations and manages their pain differently. Don't be so quick to judge because that's foolish as you don't have full knowledge about their circumstances. Everyone acts and reacts differently and that's because they have been conditioned to be the way that they are. They are moulded by their own pain and trauma whether you realise it or not. The most awkward situation is when due to prejudice two people separate and distance themselves from one another. A lot of people fall out with others over pettiness and because of pride, they never reach out to them and over time it becomes uncomfortable; you never know what they're going through and tomorrow they could be gone. You should strive to be on good terms with all those that you interact with in life.

When it comes to assumptions you should see things for what they are not what you want them to be. Don't assume too much good or too much bad but have a balanced, just view of a person especially if you don't know them well. As humans we make assumptions and then develop expectations of others, this doesn't help us because assuming things mean that we may not consider the reality of the situation. For example, we may dream to be in the life of a certain person or taken under their wing perhaps because we see a future with them or we see value in what they can provide but if they don't view us in an equal light or with the respect we deserve that means that there is a disconnect. You can continuously chase this person and force yourself to be with and around them but the love is not mutual instead you will look desperate and hopeless. You need to be able to accept the truth even if it's the harsh reality, if it means you experience emotions of sadness and upset so be it because in the long-run chasing the love and affection of those who don't mirror it back will have meant you wasted your time and effort and left yourself susceptible to heartbreak and devastation. Then again, everybody deserves to be given a chance in your life however when they come to you with the wrong energy not necessarily on one but a number of occasions then it is your cue to cut them off. The reason being is that everyone you meet knows something that you don't; they have experienced something you haven't. You are blessed with the opportunity to learn from them. The chance to apply the principles and lessons they have learned in your own life. What you will eventually come to learn is that you've done enough wrong yourself to never look down on others who've fallen off their path. We are all susceptible to making mistakes so it would be somewhat hypocritical to judge others for their shortfalls. What is worst is when we judge the fault of others yet remaining blind to our own faults.

Prejudice isn't always a bad thing and could be leveraged and used to your advantage as it leaves you being left underestimated which is a beauty in disguise because it allows you to have leverage by knowing more than you say, thinking more than you speak and noticing more than they realise. You are able to pick up on others behaviours, both verbal and non-verbal. That means whilst people are making assumptions about you as a person, they are revealing their character as a person and these samples of information allow you to form factual judgements based on truth and experience. You can't control other people, their views and their prejudice but you are in charge of yourself and can control your thoughts. One way to prevent negative preconceptions is by making excuses for the person. You shouldn't rush into thinking evil of them and interpret their actions in a negative way. They may have a justification for acting a particular way or be able to reason why they played out a situation the way they did. We may also be at fault when it comes to preconceptions due to our lack of knowledge pertaining to a matter. For instance, one evening at the mosque I made eye contact with someone and I greeted him with a simple "Peace be upon you!" and he looked at me but didn't reply so in my head I thought to myself that this man was very rude and lacked manners but I had come to that the man was mute after being informed by another brother. I guess it taught me not to make assumptions without full knowledge and that I should make excuses for people when they react in a way that isn't deemed usual because there may be a reason as to why they reacted that way (or not reacted at all in this case).

Character & Attributes

Character is how you treat those who can do nothing for you. We should strive to be honourable individuals. Honour is having a sense of principled character and personal integrity. Your true value is what you are worth to people if money and power didn't exist so your true value has a direct relationship with the character you display. Character is like a reflex action, it will show itself out eventually and true colours are revealed due to emotions being triggered. A person can only be fake for so long and their façade isn't sustainable. Character is the blend of characteristics and attributes that make up a person's personality.

Good character boils down to manners which is how you conduct yourself in relation to others and their respective situations. There are flurries of traits and features that can be learned and developed which can be benefitting for you as an individual some which I've already discussed and alluded to such as having a positive, realistic mindset, being able to take accountability for your actions, being disciplined with your work, being private and the list goes on. In this chapter, I will be looking at another set of character traits which can empower you and be useful because with a good set of admirable traits you open yourself up to more opportunities because people will want to work with you because of what you embody, your reputation and your value. On top of that, a person with good character is seen as a role model to others especially the younger people. Young people often emulate the character traits of an adult role model and the greatest thing you can do for someone is to educate them and then inspire as the highest human act is to inspire.

Honesty

In my opinion, honesty is the foundation of all moral, positive and virtuous character because it is packaged with attributes such as truthfulness, loyalty, and integrity. The truth is extremely powerful so say what you think regardless of who thinks what or who might get offended because of political correctness because then you get to express your view which allows others to interfere and debate with you which leads either a change in view or a mutual understanding which ultimately means a broadening of perspective enhancing your analytical ability. Honesty allows you to sleep like a baby at night because you are not withholding anything from anyone. Honesty isn't just about telling the truth but being real with yourself and others and most importantly not lying, it provides you with clarity in your vision of your goals and of others. When someone finds the need to lie about others, know that it is a definite sign of others' success and your failure. Honesty is a weapon that cuts through lies, deception, and falsehood like a hot knife through butter.

Be brutally honest with yourself, your friends and with anyone really under all circumstances as it reveals other attributes of yours such as loyalty. Loyalty comes hand in hand with honesty. You need to stop expecting loyalty from people who can't even give you honesty. Honesty is about transparency; being able to tell a situation as it is without avoiding details so, in essence, telling the whole truth. Honesty benefits both parties because the one who is being told the truth is able to work a solution to figure out the problem presented to them and also if the truth was withheld from the person and they were to find out later or from another person it will damage your relationship with them further and trust is lost.

Trust is the basis of all strong friendships and bonds. It is something that develops over time. It can take years to build up trust and a matter of seconds to lose it. Trust isn't something that is easily repaired either; I think of trust metaphorically like a glass, whilst intact it can hold contents inside of it, these content are your feelings, secrets and other information but once this glass is broken it cannot be used and is no longer able to hold these contents; also trying to pick up the glass and fix it may prove harming because you can get hurt picking up the pieces. People may think that they live a life of no wrong and that they are always in the right yet are faced with problems such as drama, but this drama does not just walk into your life. Drama requires participation so either you have created it, invited it or associated yourself with it. Detach yourself from negativity, achieve your goals and importantly be truthful.

You can earn trust and show your truthfulness if you:

1. Do not lie or hide the truth (to others or yourself)
2. Do not cheat
3. Do not pretend
4. Say what you mean
5. Deliver on promises
6. Give trust
7. Explain your decisions
8. Do not defend dishonesty

True honesty is when one is sincere in practices whether it be personal matters or in business. Honesty and the transparency it brings allow for both parties to trust each other which means the relationship can flourish into a stronger bond where both parties can mutually benefit. An honest person is often a sincere person. You can tell if you are sincere when you are the same person domestically and publicly with the people. If you are the same person on the outside world as you are on the inside world then it indicates you are doing things for a good purpose and not for the validation and praise from society and those who can see.

Another way to tell if you are sincere is if you take criticism with the same weight as praise. A wise man's best friend is constructive criticism because it gives them a review of themselves with pointers on where to improve to be even better as a person. If you take praise with more weight than criticism than you build ego which is toxic as it causes you to overinflate your self-importance and this can be dangerous especially when this ego reaches a level where you aren't humble and you think others are inferior to you. Huge ego puts you at a huge risk because all it takes is one event to knock reality back into you and that reality might knock you so hard and unexpectedly you wouldn't be ready. You will be similar to an inflated balloon which then has a pin pierced through it, your self-esteem will fall until you hit rock bottom and it will be a hard, gruelling task to build your self-esteem back up. On the contrary, if you take criticism with more weight than praise you build negative schemas. Negative schemas are negative cognitive frameworks that lead you into believing that you're not good enough and are incapable of achieving greatness. Too much thought into criticism can make you depressed, demotivated and also make you lose sight of your dream and purpose. Caring too much about criticism will lead to your own timely demise as it becomes a dream crusher.

Respect

Respect is a three-part process at least if you want to achieve the highest level of it.
You must:

1. Respect yourself
2. Respect others
3. Have others respect you

Respect is the consideration of others' feelings and rights. When you are respectful you understand the wishes of others and sensibly allow them to have their space and time. You need to respect yourself before others respect you because once you respect yourself you set yourself limits as a safety measure which allows you to act in an appropriate manner without encroaching on other people. Respecting yourself saves you from embarrassment and irrational decision making which leads to unfavourable outcomes that could affect you in the future.

A key element of self-respect is setting boundaries to protect your energy. A lack of boundaries invites a lack of respect. You can't afford to be understanding to such an extent that you allow everything to slide and be kicked under the carpet. Be a stand-up person and address issues there and then as opposed to letting hatred build up within you which could lead to you acting in a reckless and unprecedented manner. Being a stand-up person is about being someone with a backbone. A man stands up for what they believe in and when you stand up for what you believe in you accept the consequences that come with it; what is right is right and what is wrong is wrong. If that means you limit your availability to those who don't support you so let that be the case. In fact, you need to create boundaries otherwise you run the risk of being made to look stupid. There is a Persian proverb that roughly translates to: "Don't be too sweet you'll be swallowed but don't be so bitter because you'll be thrown up." This means expressing yourself to others in moderation and this is so you can protect yourself. Every country has a border; every house has a fence and every human should have somewhat of a guard. You shouldn't be hostile so that your ability to socialise with others is affected but you don't want to be seen as an easy target for people which will allow them to leverage power over you.

Defend your honour and dignity by avoiding situations where the topics of conversation are frivolous. When someone's name is mentioned in a gathering in a negative light and they aren't there to defend themselves, it should be your cue to pull out of the conversation and invest your energy better elsewhere. People may employ reverse psychology tactics saying things like "Oh, so you're going to defend them?" when in actuality you are just protecting your energy from the negativity present; you don't have to necessarily condone the actions of neither defend the person who is the topic of conversation. You are simply defending your right not to be a part of a session that may be filled with backbiting and slander. You are accountable for what you hear in that conversation so if something were to happen and it bites you in the back, it will be you at fault because you had the option to leave. People for some reason love to obsess over others and their business especially when it doesn't concern them perhaps it's because people have egos and want to be seen as better or because they want to displace their true emotions about their situation on another person. You may see them talk down on someone's status and the role that they have because society has brainwashed them into looking down on others. For instance, a person may have a job which is perceived as a 'bad job' by societal standards and others may ridicule them or belittle them but if we were to be wise we wouldn't knock another man's hard work and effort because once again we don't know another man's situation.

In order for you to receive respect, you can't be arrogant. Arrogance is a trait that is the polar opposite of respect. Arrogance is being full of yourself and conceited thinking that you are always right. You strut around like you know everything when you are none the wiser. On the other hand, confidence is humble, quiet and doesn't shout. When you're full of useful knowledge and share it in a manner that doesn't make the other person feel ignorant. Confidence is when you have trust and belief in whoever it may be or whatever it is, with confidence, there are high levels of trust and pride has been parked aside. Pride has resulted in people not willing to do certain things because they believe they are too good to do such a thing or they are better than that. Don't be proud but be humble and grateful for the opportunities you are blessed with on a daily basis. Once people see you as a respectful person then they admire your character and they would want to out of their own will associate themselves with you because of how honourable you are. The energy you initially exerted will be reciprocated so they will respect you, respect your view and defend your name.

Self-love

Self-love is about doing what is best for you and will bring you happiness. Self-love is often confused for being selfish but it's not selfish to put yourself first. It's encouraged and you deserve to be as good as you possibly can to yourself, to take care of yourself and to keep well and healthy. It means you understand the rights you are entitled to and to claim these rights because of the value you bring to the table. You have the privilege of being particular or picky because it is your time, your energy and your life and you should value it enough to set yourself high standards. If you are confident with what you have to offer then you should be able to choose to allocate your energy and attention to whomsoever you want. The case for most of us is the good qualities that we have are good enough for us. You have to strengthen your positivity so that it not only benefits you but that energy transcends and begins to influence others around you. Your positive influence needs to be domineering and powerful enough to resist the evil and negativity otherwise you will succumb to its influence over you. You are either affecting the world around you or you are affected by it. If you want to be successful you have got to be selfish with all opportunities and doors that open up. Take for yourself first, the give to others. Help yourself first then help others. When you are on an aeroplane and the flight attendant gives the inflight passenger announcements notice when talking about the case of an emergency how you should secure your oxygen mask first before assisting another person. You should always help yourself before helping others because otherwise when helping others you will be providing them with nothing because you have nothing or you are letting them have everything leaving you with nothing.

Saying that, it doesn't mean you shouldn't disregard everything and everyone else. Self-love doesn't mean that you don't have love for others but it means that you have a good blend of love for yourself and love for others. Gratitude is something we should look to show. You should act in a way of love. Don't count favours and do things out of love. If you are in the position to put those you love into a better situation you should do so.

Gratitude is one of the easiest ways to achieve a sense of fulfilment. Be grateful for every second of every day that you get to spend with the people you love.

Life is precious and short.

If you can walk, to a disabled person you have the world.

If you can see, to a blind person you have the world.

If you can talk, to a mute person you have the world.

If you can hear, to a deaf person you have the world.

If you have family, to an orphan you have the world.

Gratitude comes from humility. Never forget where you came from. Never forget your roots and history. A lot of our parents or grandparents were living for us whilst we are living for ourselves. How would the people from your motherland or your ancestors who lived in hard times think of your habits? We may originally come from areas of poverty where clothes are hand-washed, where there is no hot water, where the street lights are the moon and roosters serve as alarm clocks so don't get caught up in the hyped nonsense and materialistic things in life.

Sometimes it's needed to be a bit selfish but not too much. A moderate, balanced level between caring and selfish. You can't be too caring and always tend to others because you will attract damaged people because of your healing spirit; it is okay to be selfish because it will lead to your betterment which can benefit others in the long run. Be sure to have people that you can fall back and rely on too because who will heal you? Caring too much about everyone else can get you in complications that consequence in your downfall. Someone who is altruistic is at risk of being judged as superficial despite having clean and pure intentions because those judging them are filled with hate, envy, and jealousy. In the animal world, some element of care for others is necessary but for self-preservation there has to be some selfishness as well. You can be selfish yet clean-hearted but if you continue to care, care and care then it becomes second nature to you and you end up sacrificing what's good for you because you want good for others. You will feel the need to help people even if they don't need help or deserve help because this helping tendency of yours as gone way out of hand and become a routine. You trick yourself into thinking that you need to help people as if you need to pay them back. You need to be able to stop treating people as if you owe them something because you don't.

If you can help someone along the way of your journey that is one thing but breaking your neck for someone is something completely different. Once a person sees that you're willing to compromise your position for them they will try and reap as much benefit as they can from you even if it leaves you in a difficult place. Cut off the negative energies especially those which are stealing your value and resources from you. Divorce the toxicities and terminate relationships if need be. Don't be afraid about stating the facts because bringing up previous experiences is not exposing someone, it is revealing a pattern. Narcissistic behaviour is a poison that will eventually drain you mentally and burden you with guilt.

Be careful with whom you help because when the outcome results in success everybody wins but when there's a loss it will only be your loss. The more people you involve in your process the increased likelihood of failure there is because you introduce new liabilities. If you are able to do something for yourself, do it! It will be to your standard and it will potentially be more cost-effective. Just because you have love for someone or want goodness for them it doesn't mean you can help them and put them on to success. You should look to set an example for your friends and those who see you as an inspiration so pave the way, create the blueprint so they can follow it and achieve their own success independently. Everybody wants to be given a shot but don't give handouts to those who don't deserve it.

You can't help everyone. People may not be ready to reach their full potential and fear the prospect of leaving their comfort zone. They will get mad at you for giving them opportunities. From the outside looking in something may look easy but they cannot see the time, the effort and the dedication it takes to achieve what you have. They get mad because you don't do for them what you do for yourself. When someone gives you an opportunity they most likely do it out of love but this doesn't explicitly mean that they are willing to do everything for you. They didn't offer you their commitment but rather presented you with an opportunity that you had the option to take on and accept. They are giving you a chance to achieve success, follow your dreams and gain independence. So in the case where things don't go as you anticipated them to go, you have no right to blame and fault them for your failure. In that situation, they are teaching you to fish for yourself. It said that if you give someone a fish they can eat for a day but if you teach them to fish they can eat for a lifetime. So if you teach someone the technique, the art and the skill they will have learned for themselves to an extent they can apply these skills to a number of situations in a number of different environments to their own advantage. Despite that, in life, some people just can't be helped because either they don't want to contribute to their growth or they are too lazy to achieve something substantial. I have got a number of friends that I love to death but I can't build with no matter what I try because they need to initiate change within themselves.

Forgiveness

Forgiveness is when you intentionally make the decision to release negative emotions such as vengefulness and resentment that you had towards someone who has hurt you regardless of whether they are deserving of your forgiveness or not. Forgive people not for them but for yourself so you can begin your healing process. It hurts more to hold on to your pain than to let it go because it causes you self-inflicted psychological damage. You can refuse to forgive someone all you want but forgiveness is about you and not the other person. When you forgive someone for wrongdoing you, it allows you to cut them loose because they are no longer a part of your process and journey. Forgiveness removes the chip off of your shoulder. When you choose to hold out your forgiveness it will not somehow hurt them and they will not be subject to the same pain as you were that is flawed logic. I know of people who have held feelings of anger against another person for several years and all it has done is hurt them; deteriorating their own mental wellbeing. Forgiveness is for your own personal growth and happiness and it frees you from your mental shackles allowing you to live in the present moment. Forgiveness is not only for occasions where someone has done something wrong to you but also when you have done wrong to someone else. Everybody is owed apologies and everybody owes apologies.

Forgiveness begins with you and then others. The one and only thing that you are entitled to in this life is your own forgiveness. Forgiving others does reduce the burden and pressure placed upon you but forgiving yourself alleviates you from unrealistic expectations you hold yourself to. Forgiving yourself keeps you level headed and with both feet on the ground. It serves as a reminder that you are still a human and that you're not perfect and will make mistakes and that's fine so long as you learn from those mistakes. The first person deserving of all the qualities you possess is you. Stop being so hard on yourself; the same kindness and excuses you extend out to everyone else are also entitled to you. Why be so hard on yourself but so easy and forgiving on everyone else? Treat yourself the way you treat others as this is a part of self-compassion. Once you have forgiven yourself, you clear your mind and have the capacity to forgive others, move on or rekindle relationships. Forgiving others is the most common forgiveness given but there is still confusion over what constitutes forgiveness or an apology. Forgiveness doesn't mean that a person is granted the permission to enter back into your life nor does it have to mean they can't be within a five-mile radius of you but once forgiveness has happened, past emotions are put aside and the parameters of the relationship are set through mutual agreement. When an apology is given it should come from the heart as it shows sincerity. You should acknowledge what was done wrong, why it was wrong and make oath that you'll never do it to them again. The tongue has no bones but is strong enough to break or make a heart so be careful with your words. Apologising does not always mean you're in the wrong, it means that you value your relationships more than your ego. All apologies start with a simple "I'm sorry…" and end with an understanding of both parties' boundaries.

One reason why we don't forgive is that we believe that if we forgive someone we are compromising our feelings. You most likely will hold them to the action they've committed because you don't want to let go of that injustice or are expecting that they suffer similar consequences to you and feel pain in a way you have. You don't feel you want to let you off. We need to cut them loose because although they are responsible for the initial pain that we felt; we are responsible for our emotions so continuing to hold them to what they've done will ultimately lead to more harm to us because those emotions of anger and injustice will consume us potentially preventing us from flourishing as individuals. Forgive and not necessarily forget but learn a lesson. There is no need to hate them but don't allow yourself to get close enough to hurt you again.

You can't allow your forgiveness to become foolishness. You can forgive someone and yet not want anything to do with them. It needs to be understood that forgiveness is for past reconciliation and not for future reconsideration. No matter how much you resent someone and hate someone it will not change or reverse the pain you felt; you have to live with that pain. It doesn't change what the person did to you. You have to manage the trauma, pain and hurt that was created. Accept that the person did and said what they said to you. Carrying a hatred for a person will only hurt you. If you are waiting on an apology from them then you are doing nothing but holding yourself hostage to that person's apology. Yes, you've been hurt and a wound is apparent but by holding resentment it is as if you are stabbing yourself where you are cut, leaving you in more pain at the moment. The scars will be there regardless.

Humans are prone to mistakes, human nature is to make errors, and this is a fact of life. However, there is a line that needs to be drawn as there is disrespect due to carelessness and poor choice of language and then there is a violation of principles. We need to be able to forgive and oversee the minor faults in others because otherwise, feelings of hatred begin to manifest within ourselves which leads to negative consequences. Forgiveness is a two-way street so if you want to be forgiven for your sins and shortcomings then you should be able to forgive others for what they've done to us. Of course, there are some violations that cross the line and we have to take to the grave with us but otherwise, there is no benefit in holding a grudge. The human experience is short at an average life expectancy of about eighty years so there is no point wasting energy fixating on useless matters. Perhaps it would be useful to understand why a person did what they did to you instead of pulling out the victim card. Find out what events led to tension building up and what was the last straw which blew everything up. Find out if the person really meant what they said or it could've been something they said under stress and anxiety. Perhaps they were going through a rough patch in their life and were broken. Do not confuse a broken person for an evil person. A broken person can be fixed whilst an evil person cannot. An evil person causes pain, hurting others. They deliberately choose to cause chaos revealing sadistic features in their character. A broken person would never act in this way because they know how it feels to be on the other side of those actions and be the victim of emotional abuse.

Love & Relationships

Love is the intense feeling of deep affection that you have for yourself, someone else or something else. When love is between two individuals it becomes a relationship where two people are connected to each other in some way- a bond is formed. Factors such as loyalty, respect, communication, and safety help to strengthen a relationship proclaiming the love between two people.

Love is a word that is thrown around too easily causing it to lose its meaning and value. Love should be a special and exclusive thing. Don't go around using the term without truly meaning it. Nobody should use the word "love" and direct it to someone else without willingly taking the responsibility and ownership of its requirements. In an ideal world, you should be able to love people for who they are. If you like them, you like them; if you don't like them, you shouldn't mind letting them know that you don't like them as it is not a requirement for you to like them. You can have love for someone by having an appreciation for and strong liking to elements of their character but this doesn't mean you love them wholly as a person. Love is determined by your intuition. Love sometimes doesn't work out and just because you love someone doesn't mean you're supposed to be with them because the energy between two people must be aligned. A good relationship should bring you peace and not have the opposite effect, leaving you in pieces.

In order to achieve peace, you need to distance yourself from those that you love but don't reciprocate that energy and start engaging yourself with those people that love you. If a person wants to be a part of your life, they will make an obvious effort to do so. Think twice before reserving a space in your heart for people who don't make an effort to stay. Some of us are in relationships with people because we are in need of the validation that they bring to our lives, no other reason. They give us the validation that we fail to give ourselves. A healthy partnership is one in which the people we allow into our lives should be genuine and mutually beneficial, a symbiotic relationship. Never beg a person to be in your life, don't try and convince them to be in it either, not because of pride but out of self-respect. If you beg someone to be in your life then it isn't your best interest because they are not willing to put effort, dedication, and love into that relationship to make it work. It would be a shame if you make someone a priority in your lives when you are only seen as an option in theirs. You cannot control someone's loyalty. Being good to them doesn't mean they will treat you the same.

What you place your life around consistently will influence. Often you find people that are living happily and once they enter into a relationship they have changed because whilst the relationship may look good the person that they with didn't have a good mindset, spirit or heart which rubs off on them. The same goes for friendships and associating yourself with negative, gossiping and low ambition individuals. Everybody doesn't deserve access to your life hence you have to be careful who you give a key too. Two people are not directly responsible for each other's happiness. The fundamental basis of happiness starts with you. If you can't make yourself happy don't expect another person to make you happy. Another person can provide you with attention, a shoulder to cry on, support, to grow together and give each other room to grow individually. You have to make sure your energy is correct before committing yourself to a relationship. You don't want to walk around imbalanced energy. You find that you try to justify your rationale by saying that you're not the best of people. However, you don't need to announce a disclaimer for the way you behave because of the shortfall on our behalf. There is a guilty conscious and shame that can be repaired instead of being held as a weight on our shoulders. You don't want to be in a state of spiritual crippling and debilitating faith.

The problem with love is it is one of the greatest vulnerabilities of a man and has led to the emotional and psychological downfall of many who didn't understand this. Love puts you in a vulnerable position, so it is tremendously important to be careful who you allow yourself to love. Selfishness is a part of the survival mentality hence love should be given intently but also intelligently as not everybody is in deserve of your love and affection. Love soon creates attachment so even if a relationship was a thing of the past the person will forever be a part of your story. When in love you are emotional and may not think things through revealing your deepest and darkest secrets to another person but you must be prepared because even those who you love will stab you in the back and this is especially true if the love isn't mutual. Often we confuse our love for lust, especially when looking for a partner because it is in our innate disposition to go for the most attractive partner even if they don't fit the suitable criteria that makes them compatible for us. Relationships are not a bad thing especially if both sides can bring something to the table. Relationships can be sexual, platonic or professional and relationships need to be maintained because humans are social creatures and life is difficult to survive as a lone wolf; the company of others provides you with love, help, and guidance all factors which can improve happiness and other chances of success. Relationships can be of different levels and strengths; you will not have the same bond with a family member as you do with a business client. They also come with external troubles. When in an intimate relationship whether romantic or platonic you don't need to involve others as that interaction is personal and private. Everybody doesn't need to have a front-row seat in your relationship because maybe those people have envy and jealousy set in their hearts and they eventually start to take out those feelings out on you because they can't understand why it is you who reap these benefits not them. They are unable to process their own blessings as they are so fixated on what another man is enjoying.

A stable and healthy relationship is determined by three primary factors: trust, respect, and communication. No relationship is perfect but a not perfect relationship doesn't mean an unhappy couple. When you have a relationship with someone you compromise things and come together and build in order to keep each other happy. However, there is a limit to how much you should compromise. As humans, one of our roles is to not complicate the journey of others because we are susceptible to our own faults and we wouldn't want our bad character to compromise the potential of another person. You don't want to be left with the guilty conscious that a certain person doesn't achieve their potential because of the heavy influence you had on them. Not only does this leave them in a state of 'what if' but they may blame you claiming you were responsible for their reality. This ultimately means animosity in the relationship where the love is lost. Self-sacrifice is needed but don't let this be an excuse for your partner as they will take liberties and try to abuse their rights which in turn leads to you being treated unjustly and like a doormat you will be walked over.

One key to having a successful relationship and is with a vice-versa mentality where you act in a way that you would like to be treated in. An important rule of thumb that can be followed is "never do to me what you wouldn't want me to do to you." Although being simplistic such a statement holds such weight because as humans we want to see ourselves in a good position so we wouldn't participate in behaviours which would potentially be harmful to us as that would be irrational. Therefore why utilise your energy to try and block the blessings and successes of another person through your actions because you wouldn't appreciate such a thing if the roles were reversed. What seems to be coincidental and happens every time is the tables turn. Situations are truly temporary a person may be down below at one point in their life but on top of the world at another point.

All relationships go through rough patches but the strongest of them survive due to clear communication. Good communication is essential for a healthy partnership. Communication is what keeps the connection alive between people and with a weak connection you end up with a weak relationship that can be toxic or no relationship at all. Communication is about having mutual understanding and reaching an agreement after some conversations so that both partners can improve where they are lacking. Communication like anything needs to be in balance. Too much communication can come across irritating leaving your partner agitated whilst too little communication can make your partner feel underappreciated and lonely. A solid relationship is not built upon an unstable foundation.

You can respect a person who is vocal. It is honourable to be someone who is vocal in relationships because being vocal facilitates the opportunity to communicate. You can figure out each other's problems and understand them from both sides of the argument. Someone who is stand-up can voice their opinion and debate it. However, you can't respect someone who is verbal because this type of person is someone who constantly talks with no substance and value. A wise man speaks because they have something to say, a fool speaks because they have something to say. A wise man chooses to speak in order to add value to the conversation whilst a fool speaks only to be considered a part of the conversation. A wise man is able to listen carefully to what is being said and analyse the information being told so that they can take consideration of their own words. There's a difference between someone vocal and someone who is verbal. A person who is vocal is someone who communicates out of necessity to maintain and grow a relationship whilst someone who is verbal is someone who over communicates often in a toxic way.

A lack of communication will lead to misunderstanding and when communication is finally re-established between two people there is an increased likelihood in disputes and arguments due to a disconnect in a relationship that has built up over time. When it comes to an argument it isn't about winning or losing but rather the goal is achieving a mutual understanding and agreement with each other; otherwise both sides lose as the relationship has been damaged. Communication means speaking and listening. Hearing is to notice something is being said however listening is to acknowledge and comprehend what is being said. Listening is what keeps relationships healthy because a mutual understanding is achieved. When communicating you shouldn't say what you think will subdue the situation even if there is tension but tell the truth. Don't be one of those people who sugar-coats and manipulates their words in order to keep everyone happy. Communicate in a straight forward manner whilst being respectful and emotionally intelligent of others. Relationships are simple but people are complicated. Relationships work off a single law and that is to never make the ones you love feel alone especially when you are there. You can let your partner know that you're there for them through interaction and engagement as that indicates you have value and care for them. Appreciation is better showed than told.

Don't think because your communication and bond hasn't been up to par you should continue like that and be petty. The silent treatment is a form of emotional abuse. It is a tactic used to punish someone and it is designed to cause harm by making the victim feel powerless, invisible, insignificant and non-existent. Instead, speak to them and speak to them appropriately. The biggest communication problem is we don't listen with intent but rather with the intent to reply. When communicating allow them to voice their thoughts and when you decide to speak, think before you speak because it can save you a lot of hassle. Sometimes you may say something wrong or haven't said something clearly enough. Our minds are our greatest assets and hold huge power so we should use them. A wise man once said "mastering discretion is greater than employing eloquence" which means knowing what to or what not to say and remaining in silence at times proves better than speaking in a beautiful and sophisticated manner. Being able to keep the conversation simple enough for the other party to understand and explained enough for them to understand is far better than sounding over speaking so say what's necessary. One person may be able to achieve the same thing as someone else in a single sentence as opposed to a paragraph.

Someone who refuses to settle is someone who is single by choice and there is nothing wrong with that. Nobody should enter a relationship out of desperation to satisfy the standards set by society. The idea of waiting for a relationship sounds so stifling and stagnant. It is like how you are told as a child, if you are ever lost, stay put and remain in the same area because that way you make yourself easier to find. You don't want to have constant feelings of 'what if' whilst in a relationship. A relationship shouldn't take away from the chances in your life or stop you from going after your goals which you aspire to achieve. A relationship should complement and support you as a person, not prove a hindrance. The experience of going on adventures and endeavours alone is far more enriching than waiting for someone to take them with you. Of course, relationships are important and can seem nice but a toxic relationship can be a dearly cost in both time and energy which could've been spent better elsewhere. Staying true to yourself and your values and listening to your heart will indicate to you if it is timely to extricate yourself from a toxic relationship. Until you learn how to be comfortable by yourself, you'll never know whether your decision to be in a relationship is based upon love or loneliness. If you make a decision based upon love you can make a choice and decision based on privilege and not pain since you can effectively assess your needs and wants. You need to learn how to heal from one person without needing another. If you enter a relationship prematurely and whilst you are still broken then you unintentionally spread your pain, hurt and negativity with the other person. This then consequences in a domino effect because that person is holding elements of hurt now as well due to them sharing an experience with you. This means any new people they interact with will feel pain and hurt too. This leaves multiple people affected in a negative way as these people are the collateral of your pain and hurt. You don't heal to communicate with the person that hurt you but because you have a responsibility to those who depend on you whether it be your children, your parents or your peers.

Don't force relationships and don't force conversations. If the energy is correct then naturally you will be more inclined to hang around and speak to someone. If someone wants to talk to you, they will. If they want to spend time and be with you, they will. If they want to make things work, they will. However, you can't force them to do things against their will because there is no mutuality in the relationship making it one-sided which is unhealthy and exhausting for you. Sometimes they may not be ready for a relationship hence why you may not want to partner with someone and until they can fix their energy they won't be deserving of you. Don't be foolish in thinking that you will remain unresponsive and immune to the negativity and toxicity another person is carrying. Also, stop believing that you are not toxic yourself. We have a responsibility to give people the best, maintainable version of ourselves and if that is not possible then we should at least not show them the worst version of you. You don't want to ruin a period of a person's life by providing them with a horrible experiencing which leaves them scarred and with new trauma.

Relationships don't always work out and you may try to steer a relationship in the right direction but it's not destined to be. To avoid entering relationships that won't work out you need to stay aware. A red flag is a red flag; they are signals of warning so you must take them for what they are. Time and time again we will ignore red flags because as humans we are emotional so we act on the basis of love and attachment to people. When you are attached to someone you make excuses for them but there are only so many times a person can be excused. It's naïve to make us think that we are in love when it's actually lust. Life is definitely not a fairy tale. You can get exploited and used because you fell in love with words, not with actions. People don't exactly mean what they say because the truth is disguised with ulterior motives and hidden agendas. Everyone can make a mistake however it is how one responds that reveals their level of character, they need to respond with a correction. If they continue to repeat the same action it is no longer a mistake but rather a disrespectful choice. A second chance doesn't mean anything if you haven't learned from your first mistake. You need to understand what you deserve and not being treated right is not what you deserve. You can still love that person but from a distance. Let them move on and you should do so too instead of reminiscing on what could be. When you love someone unconditionally and unselfishly you want to see them do well regardless of where they are and who they are with.

Be precautionary. Don't love too deeply until you are sure that the other person loves you with the same depth because the depth of your love today is the depth of your wound tomorrow. Love leads to attachment and attachments lead to disappointments because expectations are not met. Any new relationship is filled with emotions. As the relationship progresses with your partner you allow ourselves to become increasingly vulnerable. Inevitably, you become more comfortable with them and this person slowly integrates themselves into your routine. They prove themselves compatible with you which in turn allows you to be your true self around them. This also makes it easier for you to become more dependent on the feeling of comfort and security that they provide for you. It becomes difficult to distinguish whether you enjoy them because of the security of being in comfort or the contentment of being in love. A relationship can gradually become unhealthy with encounters and exchanges becoming more toxic. That feeling that was once love slowly fades without you even noticing and because of initial thoughts and expectations on what the relationship could have become can cloud your judgement meaning that reality is distorted. We may create excuses for the other person due to the comfort we once felt from them but in reality, the relationship is making you unhappy and unsatisfied.

A negative relationship is harmful and a waste of your time but because you are afraid of going back to being alone again you force yourself to be someone who you aren't making you insincere. What has happened in this situation is you've allowed another person to have so much power over you that you feel as if you can't live without them. However, all of this doesn't mean a relationship is always meant to be perfect and fairy-tale-like because that is an unrealistic and unhealthy expectation to hold. It simply means don't allow emotions to affect your decision making because if the signs are telling you one thing but you are going against them opting for the alternative option you are allowing yourself to live a life that is upsetting.

Friends & Family

True friendship can be one of the most precious things in life it can turn two people into an unstoppable force. A friend is someone who you have a bond of mutual affection with. A good group of friends can elevate you whilst a bad group of friends could have you not hitting your targets and not achieving your potential. Friends hold a special place in your heart because you feel that they are deserving of your love. Choosing those you associate yourself with and more importantly, those whom you consider your friends is important as the right group of friends will not only boost you to grow but help you humble you. You learn so much when you pause and listen to what people have to say and when you watch how people behave; you should be able to use your set of friends as mentors for your development. You should surround yourself with people that push you to do better. Not people who indulge yourself in drama or negativity. You should be around those who just have higher goals and higher motivations. This positive energy will benefit you in rewarding you with good times. You cannot be surrounding yourself around those fuelled with hatred and jealousy because they will not bring the absolute best out of you and due to their own self-corruption you cannot bring the absolute best out of them. Hold on to every genuine person you find. This world is full of individuals driven by ego, money, and status. As a result, good souls are ruined on a daily basis. Keep your head up and be conscious of the energy you give out and more importantly the energy you connect with.

A friend doesn't need to be someone you see on a regular basis however they should be someone who's dependable. You should be able to go days without calling or texting your friend and this doesn't mean that you don't love them or care for them. It just means that you respect their space and the fact they have their own life and may not like to be bothered at every instance. The only person who looks for validation for their every move is a child. Your friends are still loyal to you, love you and care for you however they understand and respect that being a friend is about being someone that can be relied on not necessarily someone who is always all up in your business. You should feel comfortable in confiding with your friends. Some people, especially males, bottle all their emotions and feelings because they are scared of people using it against them or people telling them they should 'man up' instead of providing them with the emotional support they need. You are meant to be able to express yourself without the fear of what you said coming back to bite you and haunt you. Friends should be familiar with you and the way you act. A true friend can hear what you say without you having to utter a word. They will have spent enough time and understand your behaviour to such an extent that they can understand how you feel based on the vibe and body language you give off.

You can tell if someone has the potential to be a friend based on the energy they give you. Energy is natural. You can't change other people, you can only change yourself. When you change yourself, the people that are creating issues in your life either change with you or go away. This is because when you shift, everything around you will also shift. You then find your frequency which will attract others as they tune into your life. Friends are those who share some things in common with you. This means that the relationship is built upon a foundation. They often share a vision with you as your energy aligns. It doesn't make sense having an abundance of friends because it is impossible for them all to gel with you smoothly. Friends can see from the same lens as you yet are able to pick out things that you may not have noticed. If there are two people with prescription glasses: one with a lower prescription and the other with higher. They cannot exchange glasses and see clearer. One person's vision isn't for you and your vision isn't for them. Friends share the same vision or share visions which often contain a lot of similarities hence they can help each other as they head the same direction. There is no way that two polar opposites cans hare the same space at the same time because the energy of both will be pulling each of them respectively in two different directions. Each person is unique and has different desires and inclinations. You can't have a close friend and break up with them except that they do something that goes against your principles. We are to blame to an extent because we may condone some of that type of behaviour.

If your friends don't motivate you to level up or support you they are not your friends. Simply because you have been with someone from a young age doesn't mean anything. Some relationships are forced by our environments. You have most probably got friends that you've just met who support you more than people you have known for ages. A stranger will support you more than people you know because people you know often come from the same environment as you, they aged with you and spent large portions of their life with you so eventually when you do things which are considered abnormal for that environment they have a tough time accepting your progression and want for change. People can be afraid of the person you might become but they don't see their potential in that same light because of their own self-doubt. These same people will remind you of your past and how vital they were in your life to become the person you have become but the truth is they are just planting seeds of guilt and doubt in your soul because they fear you moving on. You need to disassociate yourself with those that you need to remind how much you appreciate them. It is time to let them go as nothing you do will ever be good enough. Leave them to their own insecurities and move on. You've done all that you could with and for them.

A family consists of the people, who support and love you. They are the people you can confide in and trust. Friends can become family and so long as they are someone that supports you and if they don't then they are not a friend but an associate. If a family member, by definition, doesn't support you then they are nothing but a relative, someone related to you by blood. Family is just like any other membership, in the sense that, it can be cancelled because if these members are perpetuating toxicity, they are not fulfilling the acceptable contract and duty as family. A family is a team where each and every person has a role to play. To be a team you have to move as a unit and you're only as strong as your weakest link. A number of relationships working together and serving a related purpose creates a unit. Unity gives purpose on a large scale where each and every person is contributing their part and serving their role to achieve the objective whatever it may be. One interesting concept I have come to understand is sometimes letting people help you, in fact, helps them and reaffirms their purpose. For instance, I have a grandmother who spends a large proportion of her time in the kitchen cooking and she doesn't like it when we decline to eat even if she hasn't started cooking because cooking and feeding us reaffirms her purpose as a nurturer even though we may see it as a burden. The understanding and analysis of a situation will be far more useful than any theory that is learned because the reality has factors that haven't been considered and theory doesn't work on assumptions. Have respect for your family and respect for the role each and every member plays because only together does a family function properly and powerfully. Each member is a cog in the wheel.

Friendships like any relationships can be toxic and you must know if your friends are genuine and if not you need to take the necessary actions to protect your well-being. Don't feel guilty bad for making a decision about your own life that may upset others because you are not responsible for their happiness but you are responsible for yours. You are not required to be friends with everyone that you meet in life. The main reason you don't need to associate yourself with too many individuals is that the one time you do something that they don't like or something doesn't go their way they switch up on you and treat you differently. This wishy-washy type of relationship has no place and time in your life. If a situation doesn't go their way and they feel some type of way about it and it makes them treat you differently it is an indication that they were never a real person to you in the first place. Their loyalty is based on how good they were feeling that day and their loyalty stops once the benefits they collect from you stop. Loyal friends are for you during the ups and downs of your life. There is a difference between someone who is for you and someone who is just with you. Some people may claim that you are their friend and they will sit back watching you make a mess of your life for their amusement. A friend is someone who shares life experiences with you and is a passenger on your journey. A friend knows that the mistakes you make affect them. Your pain is their pain; your mistakes are their mistakes and your failures are their failures. Some people will add weight to your back whilst others will help you carry your burden. A lot of people will take, take, take but never give back. They will call you asking for your assistance but when the roles are reversed they are nowhere to be found or will make excuses as to why they couldn't provide you with any support. Friendships are a mutual bond were the amount put in the amount received back.

There could be a number of reasons why you want to avoid the potential association with someone or why you may want to end a friendship. What typically seems to be the reason why friendships are ended is that people act differently towards you around certain people because they have talked differently about you to these certain people. You may deem someone to be a loyal associate or a friend of yours but the same person will not keep the same energy they keep with you with others when talking about you. I knew of a boy called Damien and to say the least he has mixed personalities so when having a conversation one-to-one he was respectful and supportive of me however whenever there was a crowd of people around he would get disrespectful and snide remarks about me and when confronted about it in private he would brush it off claiming it was all nothing but banter. Perhaps he thought making a mockery of me would be a way of asserting his dominance and get people to like him however it ultimately led to him being known for and quite disliked for his two-faced behaviour. Some people thrive off being the centre of attention and in the spotlight. They are actors simply putting on a show for everyone to see. They love being praised; it does their ego wonders. It becomes such a problem that they will create dramas so that they can remain the topic of conversation or continue being the focal point. You can easily lose all respect for someone especially when they do things like Damien did. You don't necessarily have to hate them but you no longer feel the need to associate yourself with them or say anything to them anymore.

A fake friend is your number one enemy. They are snakes. A snake is a treacherous or deceitful person. They are the worst type of person to encounter and walk the Earth. All snakes share the same characteristic of deceit and betrayal. In the animal kingdom, a snake sheds their skin between two to four times a year which allows it to get rid of its old skin and reveal new, scaly skin however they still remain a snake. Some humans and snakes are the same in the sense that they show themselves to be new, different and reformed after a period of time- the shedding process. You may meet someone, get to know and familiarise yourself with them just for them to represent the polarity of what you stand for and believe in; they then like a snake show themselves to be something else once they reveal their true selves. A snake poses a danger and threat to you. If you have ever seen a snake prey on its target you'd see that the snake doesn't immediately pounce to snatch its kill instead it observes the movement of its prey, acquainting itself with their kill even at times mimicking its movement then expeditiously the snake will launch itself gobbling the prey whole, slithering away as if nothing had happened. Similarly, a human will get to know you, learn your habits and once they have you in a comfortable position they will seek benefits and reap rewards. Once you can no longer provide them with these benefits or they can acquire more and better elsewhere they will take the new opportunity instantaneously even it means you're left for dead. Snakes have no concept of loyalty and act egocentrically. Experience with fake friends will have reverberations of trust issues. You never know who to trust. You may have been hurt many times in the past; your pain has resulted in you keeping your guard up because you don't know where new pain will come from. You don't know if something they do or say will trigger memories of pain so you don't allow them to enter your life or enter your life easily. Snakes play both sides initially. They will be friends with everybody including you and your known enemies. A snake deceives you into thinking your friends together when the reality is far from that. You may find your own friends instigating situations by telling you what another person has said about you but that only prompts you to ask yourself "why did the person who made the comments about you comfortable telling your supposed friends that information?" If your friend was truly your friend they will have committed to your side not be a messenger for messages about you. Despite that, you can't be disheartened about their betrayal of trust because when someone betrays you, it is a blessing. Imagine going through life not knowing that someone had bad intentions towards you. Be thankful their behaviour has been exposed sooner than later. Be grateful and move on. It may not be easy but remember it could have been worse. Take care when it comes to considering who your friends are because you don't want those same people who entered your life to come back and damage you.

According to the MIT Technology Review, humans are only able to extend to a best-friend circle to five platonic soul mates at once. On top of that, you can have another ten close friends. This totals to fifteen people. You are most probably revealing your deepest, darkest and most intimate secrets to them; obviously, you do this in good faith and in the hope they kept what was discussed confidential but you cannot guarantee that. Those are your fifteen close and best friends but they may not be friends with each other so if you tell one of them something you run the risk of them telling their friends who may not be your friend. A friend of a friend is not necessarily your friend. Some things are best kept secret and kept to yourself because your best friend has another best friend who is not your best friend. This puts you in a compromised situation where your confidential information is at risk of being leaked to people who you don't want to be holders of that information. However, just because you have a bad experience with a friend it doesn't necessarily make them fake. All friends bump heads but real friends bounce back. They deal with their issues because a relationship of value will not be wasted or dismissed over minor disputes. As long as a friend is loyal and honourable then you should be good. A lot of people will find that their friends are insincere and two-faced; the reality is if you knew what was said in your absence, you'll stop smiling in the faces of a lot of people. Ask yourself if your so-called friends defend your name when you are not in their presence or do they laugh along and engage with those making mockery of you? If they do then they show signs of trustworthiness and should be regarded as your friend if not it is an indicator that they aren't really your friends. You may have found yourself intentionally acting stupid, weak and confused to see how those around you act especially when in a state of vulnerability. You may have had them thinking you aren't paying attention to their behaviour and to your surprise, their true colours are shown and they don't act in a way that considers you and your well-being due to their selfishness.

One story that comes to mind about fake friends is one about two girls Hannah and Shanice who both went to the same Sixth Form College and developed a relationship as friends quite quickly over a time span of months. Hannah's birthday was approaching sometime soon. Hannah invited Shanice, Aaliyah, Douglas, Sophia, Samantha, Kristy, and her boyfriend Rayan for dinner and dessert. All the people invited to the birthday meal had met each other on previous occasions or had been friends from childhood so it was meant to be all love when they reunited. Hannah wanted to go for a meal at Nando's but the local one didn't serve halal food so she wanted to travel further out where they had a halal branch since Hannah. Shanice didn't understand why Hannah eating halal was such a big deal since she wasn't living a very Islamic life as she didn't wear a headscarf; she had a boyfriend and didn't conduct herself the way Muslims were meant to. Hannah was hurt by Shanice's comments and that started a backlash that had a chain-effect resulting in a cycle of slander, snide remarks and back-biting by both sides causing animosity. Shanice sought comfort in Samantha and Kristy who was a long-time friend of Hannah whilst Hannah was supported by Aaliyah and Douglas. Sophia and Rayan kept to themselves amidst the friction. As the time for Hannah's birthday drew nearer everyone decided to put their differences aside for the sake of enjoying the occasion. Hannah told Shanice that everybody would be making their own way to the Nando's which was fine by Shanice and she thought nothing of it. After college that day everybody went to their homes and got dressed. Later on Hannah, Aaliyah, Douglas, and Rayan met together before the time of the meal which was agreed at 6 pm. They had pre-booked a cab to take them to the restaurant without Shanice, Samantha or Kristy's knowledge. Sophia, on the other hand, knew the cab was booked but decided to make her own due to her home being relatively close to the restaurant. The group took the cab posting videos of themselves across their private Snapchat stories. Meanwhile, Shanice, Samantha, and Kristy waited and took the bus to the area of the restaurant. The group who took the cab arrived at 5:30 pm, took their seats and ordered their food without informing and waiting on the other invitees. Shanice, Samantha, and Kristy arrived at 6 pm as agreed and to their surprise; the other group had nearly finished their meal. Shanice questioned Hannah as to why they didn't let her know that they would come early and Hannah responded with an inadequate and poor excuse. Besides the matter, Shanice and the others who hadn't eaten ordered their food whilst Hannah and the rest started getting ready to go which Shanice found quite rude as a good friend would have stayed to see the meal out so they could go have dessert together. In the end, both groups ate dinner and had dessert but on two different schedules. Once everyone got home; Shanice decided to call me to vent as I am known to be someone quite consoling, thought-provoking and understanding. Shanice broke down the situation to me from the very beginning and I listened to her providing support and advice where I could. Shanice confessed a lot to me revealing information which I didn't need to know. Information that, if I was a malicious person, I could potentially ruin the life of a person. She let me know about Hannah's social life and her struggles with her boyfriend and other personal details. It didn't only stop there but Shanice decided to tell me about the financial struggles of Samantha and her family and the shocking details about the intimate life of Aaliyah; all of whom I would be sure wouldn't appreciate that type of confidential information being known to someone else. It just goes to show you should be careful who you trust and with what you trust them with. In all respects, just because you allowed someone to enter your circle it doesn't mean they will have your corner.

Look to strengthen your circle, empower your circle and elevate your circle. Your circle is the set of people that prove worthy of being your closest companions. Choose your circle wisely; you need to be around people who aren't afraid to tell you that you've made a mistake. Simply, because they have a relationship with you it isn't an excuse for them to applaud every action you make including those that can't be justified. We are humans; we are not perfect and are all susceptible to making mistakes so if our friends continue to encourage us whilst we are in the wrong it will develop desensitisation to our wrong-doing and perhaps even ego issues. Strong circles are able to point out each other's weaknesses to get closer to their strengths. A circle without constructive criticism is just a group of people telling you what you want to hear and not providing you with the support to level up. Don't let people fool you. You don't need more friends; you've got too many friends that aren't really your friends. Fewer people, fewer problems; limit the quantity around you and look to expand the quality of that circle. It is said that those around us on a regular basis have an effect on our behaviour. We pick up the habits of those around us so if those around us have self-destructive habits or generally bad habits then perhaps these traits rub off and develop within us. You're the average of the five people you spend the most time with. If you surround yourself with a circle of intelligent people you will be the next intelligent person. If you surround yourself with a circle rich people you will be the next rich person. The opposite is true also. If you surround yourself with a set of lazy people then you will be the next lazy person. You pick up the behaviours of the people which you hang around most closely with and this allows you to see similar results to them. If you want to achieve results of success then you must improve your circle or find the circle which is heading towards the direction you want to go towards as they will supplement your efforts for growth.

Improve your environment to the best extent; as the best indicator of you as an individual is your set of friends. It is okay to have multiple sets of friends but your inner circle of friends is the most important for the development and growth of you as an individual. Either your friends can be a catalyst for your growth or inhibit it. If you do find yourself having friendships with those who restrict you from development due to these individuals lacking ambition then it may be smart for you to distance yourself from them. Don't think you can be a superhero and that you can motivate and influence them because there is also a chance that you could be influenced and demotivated; in these situations conflicting energies are at work and perhaps the negative energy overpowers the positive energy leaving you in a predicament with effects such as lower levels for mood and lower levels of productivity causing you to achieve less than your potential. Simply look at what happens when you place a piece of rotten fruit beside a piece of perfectly good fruit. You will find that the mould from the rotten fruit spreads over to the good fruit and they both end up in a bad condition.

Acquaintances & Others

Humans are the most complex and unusual creatures to walk the Earth. A volume of books could be written about humans, their behaviours and how it affects you as an individual however we will only explore and expand on certain topics of significance in relation to people in this chapter. We interact with people every day even if they aren't family or friends as it's a part of life. These people are your associates, contacts, acquaintance or whatever you'd like to call them and what makes them different to your friends is the fact you owe no loyalty to each other and are only connect with each other due to forced environments and circumstances. You've got to go to school, work or whatever it may be with these people and it is guaranteed you'll have to cooperate with them and socialise with them in a civil manner. You have to learn how to manoeuvre in a space filled with different energies and try to control these energies around you. Your life will intersect with people whom you might not be fond of and due to the circumstance, you can't avoid them whether it be because of a forced environment such as them being from your neighbourhood or attending the same school as you or even if you in business with them.

This is especially notable when it comes to someone in a leadership position. A leader has to look at a group as a whole, considering everyone, not just the people they value and care for. The true measure of a man isn't by how he treats his friends but how he treats his enemies. So when a person extends themselves out to someone who they may not particularly be friends with it doesn't exactly show naivety but indicates maturity and sincerity because they see the bigger picture.

Energy is everything. Energy is attracted and is drawn from your surroundings. The last time you were inspired was by something you did, saw or felt. This then started a snowball effect of momentum which continued on. You may have also used that energy to inspire others around you too. Certain people and their toxic energy can block you from expanding, elevating and vibrating higher. The company you keep should complement your journey to a higher spiritual experience not complicate it nor contradict it. Keeping people around you that are the polarity of the way you claim to be going will hurt your progression. You will become a walking contradiction. I know of a particular individual who wanted to pursue a life of entrepreneurship and business but instead of networking and evolving his circle with those who were like-minded he associated himself with people who opposed the characteristics of successful business people. He went through a period where he lacked inspiration and since his circle couldn't cater to him in a way to elevate him so he inevitably joined them in their ways of crime which arguably threw away his chances of making it as a legitimate businessman. Energy is strong. The presence of someone else can automatically change your mood, your mind and your actions for either the better or the worse.

Energy has the power to influence therefore you need to know how to protect your energy. Protecting your energy is not just about distancing yourself from bad spirits but moving at your own pace and growing at your own speed because you don't want to rush your process and be left with poor results when you know you could do better. You have to know what your threshold is and don't let anyone set a bar for you that is beyond your capacity. Acclimation is about familiarising yourself with an environment and getting to know it for yourself so you can successfully conduct yourself in a way of success so if you try something new and enter yourself into a climate which is different from what you are used to, you will need to start from the beginning in most cases. If you start at a level that someone else is at, yes, you may achieve some success but you will lack longevity and burn yourself out quickly making your success short-lived. This doesn't mean that you shouldn't be around those who don't inspire you and motivate you, it simply means making sure you have an understanding of your capacity and slowly but surely try and push your boundaries and capacity outwardly.

Protecting your energy is about knowing what you're up against so you can look out for signs and red flags thus getting pointed in the right direction, away from trouble and hardship. Sometimes people can be intrusive with unsolicited information which you neither asked for nor wanted to know and this information can change the course of your day potentially proving perilous to your mental, emotional and spiritual well-being. People don't realise that, at that moment in time, they are playing devil's advocate trying to create a feeling that will make you experience emotions of vulnerability. You should be confident enough to tell that person that you don't want to hear what they say. Become a person who people ask permission from before speaking to especially if it is about unwarranted information. You want to have control over the information you let out and the impact that information has especially if that information was speculative or can be twisted and used against you. You meet people in life that instigate things and blow matters out of proportion forcing you into a sticky situation. These individuals, in a lot of cases, would instigate something to make the issue more profound, act as if they are there to help you and then turn their back on you when something bad happens. It is a case of the boy who cried wolf; they test you until they think they have found the boundary and they continue to push that boundary but what these people fail to understand is you see through their façade.

Often times the best move is no move at all. People do actions in hope of reactions and when those reactions which they expect aren't received it leaves them unsuccessful. Some people are freaks for attention and will go to the fullest extent to receive it. If you block them from what they want to achieve then they will quit their attempts of trying to achieve it meaning you win. People do the remarkable things for attention but to avoid putting yourself in sticky positions you should look to avoid them. They say prevention is better than cure so it is better for you to know what you're walking into when it comes to engaging with people as opposed to walking into something and having to deal with the problems and consequences. Look at behaviours, patterns, and trends. Before you argue with someone, think to yourself is that person even mentally mature enough to grasp the concept of different perspectives because if not there is absolutely no point entertaining their argument because it would be as if you are talking to a brick wall. At the end of the debate or discussion, there will not be a resolution and no progress will have been made. Some people are so stuck in their ways and there nothing you can do about their way of thinking. However, you can help yourself by understanding it's not efficient to waste your time and energy on low frequency, self-centred and close-minded people. That type of ignorance doesn't suddenly fix itself so avoid if you can and while you can.

Yes, people can be reprobate and wicked but that isn't always the problem and you shouldn't play the victim. It is all good and well blaming our environment for the product we become but we mirror one another so the character flaws we find in someone in our lives often need to be fixed within ourselves. When you see something that you dislike about someone else, the emotions that are triggered at that moment are usually the result of a personal dislike for the same behaviour within us. However, it is easier to point out the flaws of others and correct them than to take a deeper look at yourself and correct the same within you. The next time you see something or someone that triggers your anger; think about whether your dislike of that person is a result of their behaviour or in fact your behaviour. This is projecting your self-hate on to others. You don't really dislike them because of them but rather you dislike them because they remind you of the flaws in you. If you are able to consciously identify problems in others then the same ability should be used and applied to yourself and your problems.

Attention is a tool that can be used for different intentions. Attention can be used positively to raise awareness for a good cause or to benefit your brand and business but attention can also be used negatively or uselessly like when seeking attention for the sake of it or to manipulate people. Personally, I believe the worst type of person out of the list is a manipulator because they are like puppet masters leveraging themselves over others and at others' expense for their own benefit which is selfish, to say the least. Manipulators play with people's emotions to get what they want. They are the fakest type of individual. They are nothing but actors. They are fake individuals but eventually, everyone will show their true colours because even the best actors mess up a few lines of the script. They will say something out of line or do something which isn't right. These types of people are harmful especially once you've allowed them into your life so avoid them at all costs instead surround yourself with appreciators not with manipulators. People that add value not suck you of it. There are a couple of ways of firing toxic friends if you're having trouble with doing that. You can allow people to fall off by not engaging because it becomes awkward as tension would have built up from time away from each other and if they do try to force the relationship it becomes a dead giveaway of their true selves. Alternatively, you can explicitly divorce your relationship with them so they know not to contact and associate with you.

Some people you come across can be likened to foxes which are known for their cunningness and sly traits as well as manipulative character. Foxes in the animal kingdom are known for their excellent ability to catch prey through techniques that include hunting and theft. Foxes are crafty and intelligent they know what they are doing and are in no way oblivious to what they do especially when it comes to deriving benefit from other's hard work and effort. Foxes stealthily reap the rewards of others. For example, in the wild a fox will take the remnants of prey that has been killed by another predator or in urban cities foxes will scavenge through waste to eat. Manipulators act in the same way. They know what they are doing and use others' work to achieve their aims and goals. They work off the concept of exploitation where the weaker party is used sometimes unwillingly and sometimes unknowingly. I guess it comes down to the fact everyone is willing to eat but not everyone is willing to hunt. Life is filled with opportunists who in essence benefit from others' hard work and effort. They take advantage of situations and when things don't go their way they use emotional tactics to manipulate people into helping them.

Manipulators may fall under a larger bracket known as narcissists. Narcissism is a personality disorder and narcissists are known to have characteristics such as being manipulative, lacking empathy for others and having an inflated sense of self-importance. Narcissists can be compulsive, frequent liars who can liar so fluidly and remorselessly to exaggerate things to which have happened. Narcissists not only dig themselves into a deep hole but show themselves to be a draining energy force to those around them; they are vampires to your energy-sucking you dry of your energy until the last drop.

A personal trainer at my local gym was tricked into loving one. He learned the hard way that some people will use all kinds of unscrupulous tactics and lies to make them feel better. He was subject to heavy emotional abuse from a toxic relationship he was in. Originally this girl came to him depressed and crying about her looks and the amount that she weighed. This PT maintained his professionalism and didn't judge her, despite her being over thirty kilos overweight. He went above and beyond in assisting this girl, helping her overcome her depression and trained her so she could lose thirty kilos, which she eventually did. He made jokes to make her smile and did gentlemen gestures such as buying her flowers to cheer her up. He even sacrificed elements of his life such as stopping his training for a period of time in order to cater to her and facilitate her needs and development. One thing led to another and they entered a relationship officially and soon after got married. As time passed she became overly obsessed with him, becoming a control freak, she literally wouldn't allow him to leave the house and do anything from seeing his family and friends to contacting and replying to his clients. It got to a stage that whenever they were at the gym together and anyone came by to say "hello" she would get jealous and go crazy by screaming and threatening the other gym members especially if they were females. A lot of these people who were subject to this girl's abuse complained which resulted in this PT losing several clients; she defended herself saying she didn't want anyone to take him away from her as she was madly in love. On one occasion, whilst he was in her hometown, he went into a local shop where the shopkeeper let him know that his wife has a daughter and quite obviously he was shocked. When he confronted her about the matter she just laughed it off and denied the allegations claiming the shopkeeper might have mistaken a niece of hers as a daughter. As the months got on, the relationship grew even more toxic, abusive and she became controlling to the extent she would drop him off to work, at the gym, and would be impatiently waiting half an hour before he finished to pick him up. After some time they had a talk where she revealed that she did, in fact, have a daughter which left him speechless; he asked her why she decided to lie and she broke down crying explaining how she didn't want to lose him. This PT felt guilt-tripped and his kindness was taken for weakness and because he didn't want to be a bad person and abandon her so he convinced himself to stay, despite knowing that being with someone that already had a child was not a part of his dreams. She then went onto tell him that the reason for her acting crazy was due to her holding this big secret in her head. She also said that she had no other secrets to tell and that she was an open book. For a while things returned back to normal, he looked after her daughter by taking her to the park and things of that sort. Then out of the blue, the PT's partner started accusing him of cheating and she made these accusations without any proof or reasoning. He had had enough and left her as well as taking an extra step further by blocking her number and blocking her on all social media. A week later they bumped into each other at the gym and she began crying saying how she missed him but he wasn't interested however she claimed that she was pregnant! He wasn't confident in her word so after work, he went to the pharmacy to buy a pregnancy tester. Once they went home he asked her to test herself for pregnancy and not to his surprise she wasn't pregnant. She was adamant she was pregnant so he went to the store again to buy another and she re-did the test and once again the results showed her not to be pregnant. After being proved wrong she headed to the kitchen, picked up a knife and pointed the sharp-end towards her stomach threatening to kill herself; she managed to calm

down after some time. She regularly would start fights
and physically abuse him although in her defence he did
say horrible things to her but never did he hit her. After
some months through patches of roughness and
normality, she became pregnant with his child and he was
excited at the prospect of starting his own family.
However, the good times were short-lived and she would
get mad and start punching herself in the stomach which
unfortunately ended in a miscarriage. The abuse carried
on and she would react with suicidal tendencies. He even
provided her with his phone passcode to prove to her he
wasn't entertaining other females and having affairs but
this wasn't enough. At one point she found that he was
documenting the events of abuse, through videos and
notes, on his phone so she ended up smashing it forcing
him to buy a new one. On top of that this PT came to learn
more shocking information. He found that her little
nephew who would often stay with them and her
daughter wasn't the son of her drug-addicted sister but
her own son. Furthermore, she lied to his family about
how she got custody of the child and she would cry
saying that she was the boy's favourite aunty and how
she loved the boy. It disgusted him how she would
pathologically lie as well as making and encourages her
daughter to lie about her son making the little girl claim

that the boy was her cousin, not her sibling. Sadly, the PT felt as though he wasted three years of his life.

Manipulators are a type of people who fall under the category of fakes since they are two-faced nevertheless they are still humans and still have emotions. You should pay attention to people's behaviour when they are angry. When angry humans lose control over their emotions and instead of processing what they say; they will say what is on their mind. Often what is said out of anger is how a person truly felt and sometimes there are things said which an apology can't fix. A person should have to build a reputation of being trustworthy before you allow them access to intimate details of your life; they should have to prove themselves. In the meantime, stick with the ones who never let you down as they are the ones with a reputation that precedes them.

There are some indicators you can use to detect a fake person because fake people often share similar elements in their character. They could be fake if they:

1. Respect only those with power instead of respecting all people
2. Try hard to make people like them as if they have a point to prove
3. Desperate for attention as opposed to keeping some element of their lives secretive
4. Show off all the time and being boastful instead of humble
5. Gossip a lot instead of openly expressing their strongly held opinions
6. Make commitments easily but seldom keep them
7. Criticise others to make themselves look great
8. Are only nice when they have a hidden agenda

Real situations always expose fake people hence we need to pay attention to how those around us react in times of adversity compared to how they act in times of prosperity. It doesn't even have to be times of hardship; you can still be successful but due to a loss the love you receive from others will drop as you didn't live up to an expectation, these people are nothing but glory hunters.

This behaviour of switching sides can be found everywhere but is most commonly found in sports. Quite often fake people need validation from others so resort to following trends and what is popular because they don't want to seem out of place.

When you confront a dishonest, insincere and hypocritical person on their actions they quickly hide in their shells and get defensive. These people throw rocks at you and hide their hands. They seemingly try to provoke you, until they eventually do flip your switch, which results in an event of you lashing out at them and them playing the victim or you addressing the various issues and them playing oblivious and innocent. You can't have respect for them because of their poor character. They are the type of person to follow the hype and success and you don't want that sort of ingenuity around you.

Another treacherous type of person is a leech. Leeches are opportunists. Leeches live off of your successes and it's easy to spot them when it comes to getting your hands dirty and doing work. People love to enjoy the rewards and end-product whether it is spending money, partying or travelling. Even when you confront a leech on their behaviour they won't openly admit to their behaviour.

When you ask them to help you or support you they won't even if they say will. Talk is cheap. The same people that tell you that they're proud of you are the same individuals who will pass up on every opportunity to support you. You could be a gifted person and somebody could see the gift that you have and they may befriend so that they can benefit from your gift but if they're not blessed you won't be blessed either if you continue to associate with them. You have to reposition yourself from those people to receive your blessings because the type and level of energy you are projecting is different from theirs. There is a conflict.

Even though you may be positive and kind-hearted their energy could put you in disadvantaged situations. You will learn from that person, pick up their habits and worst of all you run the risk of developing their negative mindset. Leeches will suck you dry in the end. Nobody is exempt from the problems they can bring. Leeches are parasites that feed off someone else's blood. Someone who isn't contributing is parasitic. A lot of people you come across are opportunists. An opportunist isn't always a bad person. They are just someone shooting their shot and perhaps if you were in their shoes you would try to do the same. Sometimes you can't shake off the opportunists however perhaps you can use them so that you are exchanging value. If someone tries to use you just make sure you are able to get something out of them too. The benefits may not be equal to each other but it's better to have something than nothing. Ideally, any exchange should be equal on both sides so that value is given and value is received. If a person wants you to invest in something and they haven't got anything to put in then it's a bad situation for you. That person has nothing to lose and all to win whilst you have all to lose and a chance to win; if you are to lose they just walk away scot-free suffering no consequences whilst you have to put up with the pain. This doesn't just limit itself to business and money but with time, energy and effort you spend on and with others.

Once again it comes back to who you allow to enter and have access to your life because that is what impacts you, your situation and day-to-day business. Introduce people who will be of benefit to your life and most importantly remember and cherish those who already of value in your life. Some people are a dying breed and should be held on to tightly. In fact, you can organise people that you've already had experiences with different categories. The three types of people who you should never forget are:

1. **Those who helped you in your difficult times.**
   These are the individuals you should choose to connect with because they have proven to you that they are caring people with genuine intentions; often in these types of situations, the other person doesn't really gain anything from helping you so that must mean these people chose to help you out of their own love. However, this isn't always the case and we must be aware of those who may seem to be helping us but in reality, are not as they have insincere intentions and ulterior motives. It is also important to be aware of those people who count favours so if they do help you out in a situation, are they are doing in the hope that the action is reciprocated or so they can have one up on you? Personally, I have experienced situations where someone has helped me only to use it as a means to try and blackmail me because they did help me or made me feel emotions of guilt as I haven't repaid for their actions.

2. **Those who left you in your difficult times.**
   These individuals may not necessarily be bad people or have bad intentions for you but if they chose to leave you in a difficult time it teaches us a lesson so we can help ourselves should we be put in a situation of hardship again because it has been proven that these are not the people that you can rely on to help you when you are

struggling. As to the reason why they didn't help perhaps it was because of fear, different people react to situations differently. When you tell someone you are in trouble they may want to help but do not know how and are lost or due to the shock of this new information they may react by running away from the situation as they are unable to cope with the stresses.

3. **Those who put you in your difficult times.**
These are the individuals you should avoid and sever ties with because they haven't considered the consequences of their actions and the effects they've had on you meaning that they didn't value you in the first place. This person was comfortable in putting you in a difficulty and what is to say that they wouldn't do it again? This person takes liberties and is willing to manipulate situations for their benefit even if it's at the expense of another person. They most probably fit the description of a fake person, manipulator or opportunist to a tee. These people are self-absorbed and only have self-interest so learn from your mistakes and keep your distance from them and don't allow anyone like them into your space either because you don't want to be experiencing déjà vu.

People are greedy as we've already established. You can
do a thousand things for someone but the one time you
say no they would forget about everything you ever did
for them and then get mad at you like you're in the wrong
for nothing doing something for him. They will fall out
with you. They only like you for what you do for them
not for who you are. They value you for what you bring
to the table. When you are up and successful they will
stay down for you but when you are at rock bottom these
same people will be nowhere to be found. A something
for nothing transaction may be expensive costing you
your good reputation, money, time and agency. It's fair to
say not everyone will appreciate what you do for them.
You have to figure out who's worth your kindness and
who's just taking advantage. Although it may seem hard
sometimes to comprehend why some people aren't just
the way you want them to be or as sincere and clean-
hearted as you can be you need to remember you have set
an expectation. It is important to be realistic and
expectations especially those reliant on others and on
factors out of your control will most likely result in
disappointment. We all are a part of this world and you
are the main character of your story and perhaps one of
the main characters in the stories of those you regularly
interact with however you may just be another silhouette

of no significant importance in the background to another person. Preserve your energy, be careful who you share it with and keep it moving.

You can't help and teach everybody. There are some people that are just not teachable or worth trying to help. You can't teach people how to love, how to be loyal, how to be compassionate and how to be understanding. That's not your job. Don't lose yourself in the process of thinking you're doing good or being positive by teaching things to people who don't show it back to you. These attributes should be normal but societal standards have created a perception that these rather standard behaviours which aren't practiced as frequent is something abnormal, and anyone who adopts these attributes is special, when in fact our standards have been lowered to appreciate mediocrity. Normal has become rare, a dying breed at that. Keep your standards high and don't compromise on them. You should act accordingly to each and every individual not everyone is privileged to enjoy the same version of you. Learn to limit your access and apply your energy correctly. Something that is limited is in scarce supply hence has higher demand and is of more value. That thing becomes rare and highly sought after so make that thing be you.

Self-Worth & Validation

The comprehension of one's self-worth is the remedy to attention-seeking and validation pursuing. Self-worth begins with self-love. All of the symptoms of adversity we face begin with ourselves and our issues, therefore, the problems that need to be dealt with are internal and not external. Much of the way that we see ourselves has been cultivated by external measurements that have been superimposed on us by our immediate environment whether it is our family, work or customs of the city we live in. These cultures have already established a framework to define our self-worth and success. Most of the time, these measurements are rooted in external factors such as socioeconomic status, appearance, and academic achievements but rarely from internal qualities. The danger in this is that in the absence of these external validations we begin to feel like we are not worth much or lacking in self-value.

Value is such a subjective term. What one finds value in another may not hence why we as humans have different fascinations and enthusiastic over different things. One person may be a watch enthusiast and may find a £50,000 watch a valuable asset but to another person, that exact same watch is nothing but a piece to tell the time and thinks the person who buys that watch is stupid and irrational. The issue arises when a person allows their value to be determined by someone else instead of valuing themselves and treating themselves with the self-respect they deserve. If you tell yourself long enough that you are not worthy, you are invalid or you're not good enough and don't matter then you eventually you'll start to believe it and this is dangerous because you then become your own worst enemy. By repeating such statements to ourselves we begin to shape new attitudes and beliefs. Nazi Germany adopted this method through propaganda which developed negative perceptions of minority groups and this instrument was used to help acquire and maintain power for Hitler's leadership and that power led to chaos and destruction. The bottom line is external changes are not going to solve your problem because they do not address the root problem. The root problem is that you don't feel complete within yourself as an individual. If you don't address the root properly, you will continue to seek someone or something else to cover it up.

Learn to accept then embrace your differences because those differences make you the individual you are today. You possess a different combination of characteristics making you unique to any other person sharing this world with you. Embracing your differences means accepting not always being accepted. It means being comfortable with the decisions you make, which ultimately create your reality, but if you keep checking to see if people have come over to your side instead of paying attention to the ones that are already there including yourself then you are doing yourself no favours. In fact, it may be an indication that what you are engaging is not something meaningful and you are participating in it insincerely and your motive is counterproductive. This is a sign that you are not actually comfortable under your own skin. You are pretending to be an "enlightened outsider" but in actuality, you are intimately close to the very things you say you seek distance from. It is most probably an issue of insecurity.

Insecurity stems from a lack of self-love which has an effect on a societal level because people are no longer leaders and the number of leaders being produced is at an all-time low. People rather follow the hype and trends so they remain cool, maintain their image and still be seen as influential and accepted figures. If self-love is on the unremitting decline then the container for self-hate expands. Self-hate comes from a lack of self-love because when you love yourself you never feel inferior in front of other people's accomplishments and in fact feel comfortable in championing others so they can better hit their targets and achieve their goals. This is because you understand that supporting them doesn't take anything away from you and what you are doing. Self-hate can be heavily associated with a synergy between ignorance and arrogance. At the root of arrogance is self-hatred which is the causation of self-imposed limitations. You fail to acknowledge your true value due to the fear someone else's value overshadows you.

When you shrink in front of someone else because you perceive them to be better than you it is a form of self-hatred because if you truly believed in yourself and confident with you and your talents you will never shrink in the presence of anybody no matter how great they are. You will come across many great people in your life, in fact, everyone has certain things they are great at or great for whether it be having great influence and power or great knowledge or great people's skills. Every time you meet someone who's considered great whether a celebrity or a specialist in their field you can appreciate their greatness but not to such an extent you feel yourself to be inferior. Everybody who walks this Earth is a human just like you; they breathe like we breathe and bleed as we bleed. They have their own shortcomings and so do we. Don't let someone else's status suppress your own abilities so that you feel unvalued. Even if we do receive validation it will only end up as us being placed on a pedestal. The loneliest place to be is on a pedestal. No mercy lives there. No understanding. No compassion. Only the expectations of perfection live there. Your humanness is not accepted let alone celebrated there. The most precious people in your life will be the ones who see and accept all of you: the good, the bad and the ugly. The ones that truly love will accept you as a whole package which includes mess, vulnerability, and flaws.

Once you discover your worth you unearth your happiness as your happiness was hiding in the shadow of your difficulties. Self-worth which is the determination of one's value based on introspection and insight of one's beliefs. The discovery of one's self-worth triumphs a person's problems of the lack of self-love, self-hate, delusions of grandeur and the list goes on. Self-worth can only be found through independence because with the reliance on someone else you never uncover who you really are therefore the power of independence allows you to experience life by yourself and it liberates your raw internal qualities. Self-worth should be determined by internal factors, not external factors. Not your wealth, career, achievements, appearance, social circle or anything of that sort. Ask yourself if all of those external factors were to be stripped from you would it take the "you" away from you? A lot of dissatisfaction comes from expectations of being in possession of something whether it be money, status or another person because once we acquire that which we thought would bring us happiness and contentment doesn't leading to us being angry and frustrated. You can't allow your happiness to be contingent on anything or anyone other than yourself. Allowing yourself to be defined by your external factors will leave you with a feeling of worthlessness and emptiness. Self-worth is measured by inherent qualities, the things no one can take away from you.

The end result of a lack of self-worth is that you believe that you deserve the treatment that other people are giving you. You could be deserving of gold but settle and accept copper. What tends to happen when you believe that you are not good enough is you lose confidence and that results in you actually not being good enough because your performance and strive dwindles. Don't make your self-worth contingent on people being able to recognise it. People may see through a superficial lens and overlook a lot and just because they don't see your qualities, it doesn't mean your qualities are not there. It's not your fault they can't see your worth it's their loss. Two people are not directly responsible for each other's happiness. The fundamental basis of happiness starts with you. If you can't make yourself happy don't expect another person to make you happy. Another person can provide you with attention, a shoulder to cry on, support, to grow together and give each other room to grow individually.

Stop attaching your self-worth and value to the way another person engages with you. A person may feel because another person loves them that they are valuable. People may measure their self-worth based upon how much attention they receive so this leaves a person in a need for attention because their validation is dependent on it. This problem with this is when the attention stops they feel worthless. Someone may have thought of themselves as beautiful and they may enter a relationship and no longer think they are beautiful because in the absence of their partner's opinions and validation they feel worthless because their value is not spotted. Validation is something we seek without thinking nowadays. For instance, a housewife may spend a day cooking and cleaning the house so that the husband can come home to see it; the wife in this situation is waiting on the husband to validate her and her actions instead of her giving herself a pat on the back for her contributions and efforts. In another situation, a female may dress well and put on make-up just so her husband can validate her looks and confirm that she's beautiful as opposed to her being grateful and self-validating herself being proud of herself and her beauty. Another way in which we look for validation which is so natural to us is by telling other people what we are up to and what we are about to do. If you are about to do something that means it hasn't been done, it is just a plan. You never let the left hand know what the right hand is doing. You don't need to prove to people that you are doing something; if anything you show them what you have done. You build a track record letting your results speak for themselves. When you write a CV you don't include things which you thought of doing or fill it with ideas of yours but instead, you fill it with things which have been actioned and tasks which are in progress and in the works.

You don't want to be put in a position where you need others to affirm your feelings. You may find yourself having your feelings validated by others and you most likely do this unconsciously through throwaway comments and rhetorical questions. You don't need those around you to confirm the emotions you've experienced; instead, you should be able to accept these are the emotions you have and if they are unfavourable you should identify the root cause of these problems and work on a solution so you are in a positive state. We are all our own individuals and we shouldn't allow the opinions of others to have the power of dictating our choices. I have personally seen way too many kids sacrifice their mental health for their parent's pride and dignity being forced into career paths they are not interested in just so that their parents can show a face to the community. In the case of children following the career paths heavily influence by their parents, the children are looking to seek the validation and approval of the parents and the parents are looking for approval from the community. People nowadays need validation and approval of their behaviour. They won't do what they want and desire to do because they are afraid of the opinions of others but at the end of the day, there is no pleasing everyone. There will always be somebody who has something to say and people will always be critical and put their two cents in. To condense one of Aesop's fables: about a father, son, and donkey. They all went walking through a village and the people were criticised for not riding on the donkey being called stupid. When the son rode the donkey and the father walked the son was criticised for having no respect. When the father rode the donkey and the son walked the father was criticised for having no mercy. When they both rode the donkey the two were criticised for putting such pressure on the donkey showing no compassion. The moral of the story is there's no pleasing everyone. It is best to focus on yourself.

There are two reasons why we look to be accepted and these are to do with social influence. Informational social influence (ISI) is where one looks to change their opinion because they believe what the majority and others believe or do is informationally correct. Facts are facts and numbers don't lie so we wouldn't be wrong to adopt the opinions and answers of others based on information. However, problems arise when one loses faith in their talent and ability due to getting too obsessed with the statistical chance of them achieving something. You don't want to be in a case where you jeopardise your plans and future because others may be doing what is assumed to be right or where you don't believe in your ability second-guessing yourself flirting with thoughts of doubt and fear. The other type of social influence is normative social influence (NSI) where someone adopts the opinion of others because they believe what they are doing is normal. This is the most devastating social influence because it is because of this that so many dreams were dampened and lost. As mentioned before in this book each and every individual is unique with their own skill-set and talents so to accept that you're a part of the majority and adopting all of the majority's views would be foolish. If everybody acted in a way that is recognised to be normal then there would be no innovation, growth, and development; we wouldn't enjoy the convenience of technology and so much more.

When we are not accepted it means that we have been rejected. The more rejection we get, the more we grow, the more we learned and the closer we are to our outcome because if we can handle rejection then we'll learn to get everything we want by our own means as opposed to acquiring what we desire through the aid, handouts, and assistance of others. When you are not looking for validation you couldn't care less about the thoughts and opinions of others. You will get accustomed to rejection.

The fear of rejection is naturally designed to save your life in very specific circumstances which are crises not to become your life in every single circumstance. Don't live to please anybody but ourselves because being altruistic all the time can lead to us being limited in options simply because we gave away those opportunities to others who take those opportunities for granted. The moment that you let go of who you think you have to be and allow yourself to be the person you actually are, is the moment where you reach epiphany and realisation of you and your true talents and abilities. Your desire to be liked drops because you make room for self-acceptance. Your life also becomes easier because you no longer have to keep up and maintain these different appearances and facades. You are who you are which means people will have to like you for who you are. One way you can do this is by keeping busy. Productivity and action is a solution to not needing validation from others because if you're doing something and working towards a goal then you have no time and energy to worry about what another person thinks of you as you're invested in your own affairs. Don't be afraid of losing people in the process by focusing on your own business. What is more frightening is the prospect of losing yourself trying to please everyone around you.

One of the most dangerous people on Earth is someone who is seeking acceptance. They don't think their own thoughts and they don't and they don't feel their own feelings. They make their decisions based on what others do. They are followers like sheep who follow their shepherd or follow what the person in front of them does. It is not uncommon for a human to imitate the behaviour of their peers or those with perceived status. As humans, we want to feel accepted and valued by others so we may find that we adopt the beliefs of others so we don't seem dissimilar to them. We feel empowered when others support us because we feel as though we are a part of something bigger; our actions become actions not based on rationale but rather actions based on the validation the act will bring. We become puppets to behaving in a way that pleases people. This feeling of acceptance can be addictive. The trouble with this is that as individuals we aren't considering what is best for us and we behave in a way that we don't care for the consequences of our actions even if it is at the expense of others. The most devastating thing is a person becoming desensitised, lacking emotions such as compassion and sympathy so in the situation they act in a way that hurts someone they love they will not realise. This affects relationships and some things cannot be forgiven or forgiven easily all due to mindlessness.

Focusing on impressing other people all of the time can take a toll on one's mental health whether it is to impress the opposite gender, a manager at work or even family at home. The reason this takes a toll on their mental health is that often when people take action in trying to impress others they usually do it get a reaction from others and get acknowledgement from them so they can be noticed and feel included however if they don't get the reaction they want it then it proves destructive. The person feels like they are missing something within themselves which leads to a lack of confidence and motivation causing them to not be productive and function effectively. They need to stop thinking about what will cause other people to gravitate towards them and look to give themselves a stamp of approval as opposed to looking for it from someone else. Anyways, trying to impress others is futile. You cannot keep up with others so you need to compete with yourself. It is you versus you at the end of the day. There will always be someone who has more money than you; there will always be someone who is more attractive than you. You must try and better yourself and do better than you did the day before because that is an improvement and improvements over a span of time equates to growth. Eventually, you will reach a level of self-contentment and be proud of yourself when you look over your accomplishments and success.

Trying to impress others can also be very expensive causing you to live outside of your means. I personally know of someone who is always having car troubles. He owns a really nice, expensive, German car however the car was getting old and didn't work how it once used to and the car was regularly in and out of the garage or on the back of a tow truck. It got to a point where it was affecting his work life and his job was at risk due to the number of times he was either late or absent. When I quizzed him about his car and why he was dying to keep it. He told me that he couldn't be seen driving a cheaper car because of what it might do to his reputation. When living extravagantly whether it is with new cars, big houses, expensive watches, designer clothes or even fine dining when these things affect your livelihood then you are doing something wrong and you are doing things for the wrong reason.

There is absolutely nothing wrong with having the finer things in life however it becomes a problem when it gets in the way of what's best for you. Truly people couldn't care less about what you are doing or the lifestyle you portray, in fact, these same people if anything can grow to become jealous of that lifestyle. We are all chasing the finer things in life. We feel special with these things but we need to see who we are without these things. Who are you without these material objects and are you empty without them? Is your worth determined on the watch you wear or the car you drive or the bag you tote? Simplify things and see what you are left with when stripped naked from these material objects; this reveals to you who you truly are because then you are left with only your raw character.

Good character holds so much significance because it stays with you eternally. The moment you realise how quickly people forget the dead is the moment you will stop living to impress people. Think about how a dead corpse is referred to at the burial. A dead person is no longer identified by their name but as 'the body'. The lesson you can learn is don't let anyone hinder your betterment, peace or happiness because when you pass away you may not be anything but a distant memory. When you die people won't remember you because of the material things you had but they will remember you based on memories they shared with you, the interactions they had with you and the things you did. Our character remains long after we pass so focus on that.

I think a lot of attention-seeking and the desire for validation boils down to the fact people want attention and recognition. Attention is heavily overrated and nowadays it's common for people to mistaken the attention they receive for success. Attention is seen as something which brings validation however true validation is self-validation because you eliminate any energy which isn't in line with yours and instead you attract those who accept you for you and these people accept or respect your beliefs and way of thinking. Attention can be monetised especially in a digital era but that only covers two of four aspects of wealth financial wealth which is money and social wealth which is status. Someone who gets a lot of attention may still lack freedom and health which is related to happiness and fulfilment. It is why you see so many social media influencers and celebrities with depression and emptiness because although they may be rich and famous they still have feelings of emptiness and lack of purpose as well as the extra pressures from fame such as stress. Perhaps it is because from a grass-root level it has been told to us the norm is to compare your success to others whether it was at school and comparing grades to work and comparing salaries and lifestyles. Human nature is to be competitive and this is a blessing and a curse because competition can encourage us to strive and do better but on the flip side, it could be toxic for us resulting in us always having to prove a point. Some individuals may try to convey their arguments through a discussion and whenever they are countered by a valid point from the other side they may adopt characteristics of being loud. They are eager to be heard because they believe how loud we are is correlated to how successful their point has been portrayed; this behaviour is a consequence of having a point to prove to somebody else but not having a way to prove it. In reality, our results speak so we shouldn't have to.

Acknowledgement and validation are the two idols that every narcissist bows down to and seeks for religiously. Social media is pushing us all towards these things; we seek to get noticed by others by receiving the most likes and comments through social media because we associate the amount of interaction we receive to how valued we are which reaffirms and validates our behaviour. We must reclaim our hearts from the enslavement of our ego; we should look to redirect and our energy and devote ourselves to our purpose and goals. Social media in and as of itself isn't a problem but it is the toxicity that people input in it which causes problems. People feel some kind of security and protection hiding behind a screen and being able to voice opinions and say things which they wouldn't otherwise especially in front of the people they say things and talk about. People act in a way to get likes and views. I've seen people using social media where people harass people for no reason. People, especially adolescents, like to give off a persona of confidence but often due to their immaturity confuse it with being rude. I've personally seen teens be rude to shopkeepers who are doing nothing but their job. The reason they do this is because they want attention and approval, they want likes and views but what are likes and views when you sacrifice your dignity and respect? What are likes and views when you're hurting feelings or scaring someone? What are likes and views when you disappoint people who thought so highly of you?

On social media, people paint this picture of their life being the most amazing thing as if they are free from issues and imperfections. Don't believe the hype! Everybody has moments that they are happy and on top of the world as well as moments down, depressed and at rock bottom. It's a part of life and obstacles are overcome with some thinking and action. People concern themselves in what other people are doing, where they are going on holiday, how happy their relationships are, how many friends they have, what clothes they wear or cars they drive but social media is only what the user wants his followers to see. One way to think of social media is as a highlight reel where a person only includes the parts showing all the fun, enjoyment and memorable moments. Don't compare your real life to someone else's controlled online content. Social media has created jealous behaviour over illusions. Some people are envious over relationships and lifestyles that do not even exist however people remain foolish going about their life none the wiser. They compromise their relationships over what they think could be and they flirt with an idea which is nothing but a fantasy. The grass isn't always greener on the other side. On the other side, there could just be a filter. How often have we messed up something good by looking for something better just to end up with something worse?

We live in an age of envy where envy is taken to extremes. People are generally dissatisfied with their lives because they can't achieve the lifestyle they want but which they see others have. The compare and contrast illusion is easy to get caught up in. It is easy to look at someone else's outcome and results. However, you don't look at the type of work that they've done. You don't look at the time and hours an individual spent studying and cultivating their mind to achieve what they have. It is unfair to both them because you don't comprehend and appreciate the process that they've been through and obstacles they've had to overcome and it isn't fair to you because by doing a comparative analysis you are not valuing and appreciating your own process. Social media has created a microwave generation where people expect things to happen instantaneously. A lot of influencers promote that which is unrealistic and unachievable for the masses and the masses are deluded forcing themselves to meet expectations of how they should look and how they should behave. Often these influencers are not transparent with things such as make-up, plastic surgery, rented cars and sponsored holidays professing it's their lifestyle when it really isn't.

In life, things aren't always what they seem. Don't take everything at face value. Often times when meeting someone we're a fan of or respect, we find that their personality is the absolute antithesis of what we may have thought it would be. A lot of these role models we see lead a double life; they are one person in front of the camera and another person in front of the camera. I remember one summer I went to a famous food festival that attracted festival-goers from across the country including social media influencer and B-list celebrities. I was working at a stall with one of my uncles and his friends representing his brand. My job was to simply interact with people potentially interested in what we were doing, simply network by interacting with different opportunities so that we could increase the brand value. At one point I came across a YouTuber and social media personality who is arguably famous and I attempted to make conversation but I noticed this person despite giving off a confident and happy persona on social media was, in fact, someone who is shy, nervous and lacked social skills. I could tell this by the low tone in his voice, his body language gave off an uncomfortable vibe facing away from me and he couldn't make let alone maintain eye contact with me. So despite coming across as an approachable person conversing with him was more of an awkward experience.

It just goes to show even celebrities and social media stars who paint their lives to be picture-perfect; having everything in order may have problems and a life of chase. There is always more to it than meets the eye.

Acknowledgements

I developed a fascination for self-help books when I initially dabbled across some business and management books from my dad's collection. At the time, I didn't even know that self-help was a genre since I was only fourteen but nonetheless what intrigued me the most was the practicality and relevance of its content. Some months later, my uncle lent me a psychology-related book on reading behaviour through body language and facial expressions. To date, it is the best book I've ever read. Reading self-help books became a pleasure of mine and I am not the type of person to read for leisure. It became addictive. I just found it taught me so much information that is useful for the real world. Fast-forward three years who would've guessed I'd be writing my own book.

I started writing this book the week leading up to my end-of-year exams which were at the end of March. Originally I began compiling a huge document filled with my thoughts then I categorised these thoughts into sections and continued building and sectioning. I spent the majority of my free periods and most lunch breaks in the dedicated study rooms working and crafting this piece of work when I really should've been revising. Even after the exams I kept to myself and continued adding volume to this piece of work. Time passed and I broke up for summer holidays and I spent huge portions of my day and even spent many nights sleepless just to complete this book. I made sure every sentence was written with a fiery passion and I made sure that I could provide the reader with the best value I could.

I kept this book a complete secret and only after I'd finished compiling a substantial amount of the content did I tell a few people. The response I received was negative and I could tell by their demeanour and facial expressions. They pretended to support and either lied through their teeth or spoke to me sarcastically. I think they believe I don't have it in me to see this book through but funnily enough, I was very disciplined and determined despite questioning if it was worth it and flirting with the notion of quitting every day. A lot of people still won't know about this book until its publication date and I'm sure they'll be in for a shock, hopefully, a pleasant surprise.

Aside from those contributing their negativity I have to thank some of those who believed in me, had trust in me and kept me motivated. First and foremost I give thanks to God for giving me the blessing of seeing the light of day after every night I went sleep as it served as an opportunity to continue this body of work. As for people, I would like to thank my Dad because he is one of those people you can sit down and have an insightful conversation about the topics they don't teach you at school. He helped me expand my mind and see things from a different perspective and without that; I wouldn't have been capable of writing this book. My biggest motivation to write this book is my Uncle H as he's my biggest inspiration and although he's my uncle he plays the role of a big brother to me. He is one of the only people I could go to and speak unfiltered and truthfully to without feeling judged or under pressure. I would also like to thank my social media following for their constant support and love. I find it weird how people you know from childhood fail to show the same support as a complete stranger. Finally, I would like to thank myself (in the least vain way possible) because I never thought I'd become an author, it's just something I've never considered but here I am at seventeen years of age publishing my first book.

Anyways, I hope you as a reader enjoyed reading this book and you found it so beneficial that you'd read it again. I tried to write this book from the heart with the knowledge of the mind. I wanted to create an urban self-help book that was unique and not clustered with sophisticated metaphors that could lose the average reader. I wanted to create something that could be commercially understood and applied. Forgive me if this book didn't benefit you and if there is anything in the book you want to clarify, debate or discuss with me then feel free to contact me via email or social media. Much Love!

48420359R00122

Printed in Poland
by Amazon Fulfillment
Poland Sp. z o.o., Wrocław